The scope of the report

This report provides updated statistics for 50 indicators which between them portray the key features of poverty and social exclusion today in Great Britain. Whilst income is the focus of many of the indicators, they also cover a wide range of other subjects including health, education, work, and engagement in community activities.

The report is the fourth in the annual series *Monitoring poverty and social exclusion*, with the indicators updated for an extra year's data. In most cases, the latest data is from either 2001 or late 2000, the main exception being the data on income distribution (for which the latest official statistics are 1999/2000). Each indicator is presented on a single page, and comprises two graphs: one showing how the indicator has changed over time and the other typically showing how the indicator varies between different groups within the population.

As in previous years, the indicators are grouped into six chapters. The four central chapters divide the population by age (children, young adults, adults and older people), an initial chapter looks at income and a final chapter looks at communities. Within each chapter, the indicators are grouped by theme, as summarised in the table below.

	Income	Children	Young adults	Adults	Older people	Community
Income levels	✓					
Income dynamics	✓					
Economic circumstances		✓	✓		✓	
Health and well-being		✓	✓	✓		
Education		✓				
Social stability		✓				
Barriers to work			✓			
Exclusion from work				✓		
Disadvantage at work				✓		
Vulnerability					✓	
Access to services					✓	
Social cohesion						✓
Crime and its costs						✓
Housing						✓

Executive summary

For the first time since we started producing these reports in 1998, the number of indicators which improved over the latest year clearly exceeds the number which got worse. Many of the education, housing and health indicators have continued to improve, and others appear to have started to change for the better. The main indicators which continued to worsen were the number of older people receiving support from social services and the number living in temporary accommodation. On the latest official data (1999/2000), the numbers on low income remained virtually unchanged.

As a broad generalisation, the poorest in society appear to be sharing in the general improvements. But, on most of the indicators, significant inequalities continue to exist, with no signs that these are diminishing.

Continuing improvements in education...

The proportion of those leaving school with no GCSEs above a grade D fell by 20 per cent during the 1990s. The proportion of 19-year-olds not qualified to NVQ level 2 shows a similar pattern. The proportion of 11-year-olds failing to achieve level 4 or above at key stage 2 in English and maths has fallen by a third since 1996, and these improvements have been shared across all types of school. School exclusions continue to fall sharply from their peak in 1996/97.

...in housing...

Levels of overcrowding continue to fall and have halved over the last decade. The number of low income households without central heating has reduced by a third over the last five years. The number of mortgage holders in serious arrears continues to fall sharply from its peak in 1993.

...and in some aspects of health...

The number of accidental deaths of children continues to fall and has now halved over the last decade. Suicides amongst 15- to 24-year-olds in England and Wales have fallen by a third over the same period. The number of births to girls conceiving before their 16th birthday has now fallen by 20 per cent since its peak in 1996. Having been rising for much of the last decade, the geographic concentration of premature deaths fell in 2000.

Other health indicators – babies born underweight, obesity, long-standing illness/disability, risk of mental illness – have not changed significantly over recent years and our indicator of treatments for drug usage has been on an upward trend.

...but continuing problems exist...

150,000 pupils each year still fail to obtain any GCSEs above grade D, and 25,000 still get no grades at all. Nearly a quarter of 19-year-olds still lack an NVQ or equivalent and almost a tenth lack any qualifications at all. At any point in time, an estimated 160,000 16- to 18-year olds are not in education, training or work.

The proportion of elderly people aged 75 and over who receive support from social services to help them live at home continues to fall, and is now two-thirds of what it was at its peak in 1994. County councils

Contents

and unitary authorities appear to support far fewer households than either urban or Welsh authorities. The number of households in temporary accommodation continues to rise sharply and, at 80,000, has nearly doubled since 1997.

...and significant inequalities remain

Key stage 2 results in schools with a relatively high number of children on free school meals continue to be much worse than in other schools, and the concentration of poor children within particular primary schools continues to increase.

Underage conceptions are concentrated in the manual social classes (IIIM to V); babies from these classes are more likely to have a low birth-weight, and women from these classes are more likely to be obese. Unskilled manual workers are $1^1/_2$ times as likely to have a long-standing illness or disability as professional classes. The poorest two-fifths of the population are $1^1/_2$ times as likely to be at risk of a mental illness than the richest two-fifths.

Pensioners who are mainly dependent on the state pension and other state benefits are still three times more likely to be without a telephone than other pensioner groups and twice as likely to live in badly insulated housing than the best-off pensioners.

Whilst the latest British Crime Survey statistics show a continuing fall in the number of burglaries, those on low incomes are both much more likely to be burgled and much less likely to have household insurance, leading to obvious difficulties in replacing stolen goods. They are twice as likely to report that their quality of life is significantly affected by fear of crime and almost twice as likely to feel very dissatisfied with the area in which they live. Fear of crime is particularly high amongst Asians.

Black Caribbean pupils are still four times more likely to be excluded from school than others, and young black people are seven times as likely to be in prison.

Finally, 1 in 6 of the poorest households still do not have any type of bank or building society account, compared with one in twenty households on average incomes.

As of 1999/00, the number on low incomes remained at an historic high...

One of the preferred indicators of the extent of income poverty used by both the EU and the UK government is the number of people living in households with less than 60 per cent of median income (after housing costs). In 1999/00, there were 13.3 million people below this threshold, compared with 13.4 million in 1998/99. This number has remained largely unchanged since the early 1990s, after having doubled during the 1980s. London has the highest proportion of poor people of any region in England, but also has the second highest proportion of rich people.

...although disappointing, this lack of change is perhaps not surprising...

The Government now has a number of major policy initiatives in place for tackling income poverty, including the national minimum wage, the working families' tax credit and the minimum income guarantee for pensioners. However, the working families' tax credit was only introduced in late 1999, the minimum income guarantee (when introduced) was not at a level which would move pensioners above the threshold and many of those on the national minimum wage could still be below the threshold.

...but it is worrying...

Children continue to be more likely than adults to live in low income households, with 4 million children living in households below the 60 per cent threshold, and with 2 million living in workless households. Numbers fell by 300,000 in the period 1996/97 to 1999/00, meaning that the Government's target of lifting 1.2 million children out of poverty during its first term will only have been achieved if there were further falls of 900,000 in 2000/01. Both the Government and outside observers will have to wait for the official 2000/01 figures (likely to be published in July 2002) to see if such a reduction has actually been achieved.

...and certain groups of the population are a particular concern

Half of all lone parents do not have paid work and more than half were on incomes below 60 per cent of the median in 1999/2000.

Around two-thirds of heads of households in social housing do not have paid work at any point in time, compared with one-third in other tenures. Three-quarters are on weekly incomes of less than £200 compared with one-quarter of residents in other tenures.

Unemployed people without children are not directly benefiting from the Government's current major policies. Indeed, at 20 per cent of average earnings, the levels of income support are at an historic low, down from 30 per cent in 1983.

The overall number of people who would like paid work is much higher than those officially unemployed (4$^{1/2}$ million compared with 1$^{1/2}$) and, whereas the numbers officially unemployed have halved since 1993, the number who are 'economically inactive but would like work' has remained unchanged.

Since its introduction in April 1999, the number earning below the national minimum wage has dropped sharply, from 1$^{1/2}$ million in 1998 to $^{1/4}$ million in 2000. But a somewhat different picture emerges using thresholds which are above the level of the minimum wage but still a low rate of pay. For example, an estimated 1$^{1/2}$ million employees aged 22 and over were being paid less than half male median earnings (around £4 per hour) in 2000, compared with 2 million in 1998. Because substantial numbers of people are now paid at the minimum wage or just above, the precise level at which it is set is clearly crucial.

Issues for future evaluation

The overall conclusion of the analysis in this year's report is that, whilst many of the problems of poverty and social exclusion continue, there are a number of promising signs. Many of our indicators improved over the latest year and the Government has introduced a wide range of initiatives to tackle the problems. From a monitoring perspective, the two key questions are first, whether the initiatives are collectively sufficient to address the scale and depth of the problems over time and, second, how successful they are in helping the more disadvantaged to catch up – or at least keep up – with the rest of society.

Monitoring of overall changes based on authoritative and timely data

In last year's report, we discussed the importance of monitoring based on the net numbers below low income and other thresholds rather than the gross numbers lifted above by particular government measures. This is because the net numbers reflect what has happened once all factors have been taken into account, rather than just the marginal impact of a particular policy.

Monitoring of the net numbers requires authoritative and accurate statistics in a timely manner and we discussed the problems caused by the fact that official data on the numbers on low income is always 18 to 30 months out-of-date. As well as making it difficult for any independent observer to evaluate in a timely manner, it makes it equally difficult for government itself to do so.

This problem has now been exacerbated by difficulties in obtaining data about the extent of low pay. Whereas this data used to be available three months after the relevant surveys, doubts that have recently been cast by the Office for National Statistics on its accuracy mean that this delay is now up to nine months. Importantly, the data itself is no longer being made available to outside researchers, who instead have to rely on whatever analyses government statisticians decide to undertake. This is a cause for serious concern.

Monitoring of the differential impact on different groups

As our analysis demonstrates, whilst people who are disadvantaged are generally sharing in any overall improvements, there are few signs that the extent of inequalities is diminishing. This reinforces the need for any evaluation of policy to cover its effects on the more disadvantaged as well as in the aggregate. The Government's endorsement of this view, as set out in the National Strategy for Neighbourhood Renewal, is to be welcomed.

The problem is that there is no simple definition of 'the disadvantaged'. For example, whilst the most deprived wards in the country contain proportionally more poor people than other wards, they still only contain a minority of the total number who are poor. Monitoring the differential impact on different groups in such areas as health, education and housing should, we suggest, be an important theme of the Government's own monitoring and will continue to be a major theme of ours.

Summary of the poverty and social exclusion indicators

The table lists each indicator, together with the numbers of people affected, the variation across groups, and the trends over time

Indicator	Trend		Approximate numbers affected in latest years	Variation across groups
	Over the medium term	Over latest year of available data		
Poverty and low income				
1 Gap between low and median income	Steady	Steady	N/A	
2 Individuals with low income (below 60% of median income)	Steady	Steady	13 million (after housing costs)	In two-fifths of households the head is of working age but not in paid work; in two-fifths the head of the household is in paid work; and in one-fifth the head of the household is over sixty.
3 Intensity of low income (below 50% of median income)	Steady	Steady	8½ million (after housing costs)	Lone parents are twice as likely as couples with children to live on low incomes and three times as likely as adults with no children.
4 In receipt of means-tested benefits or tax credits (working age only)	Improved	Improved	4 million	Sick and disabled people are the largest single group of working age on means-tested benefits.
5 Long-term recipients of benefits (all ages)	Improved	Steady	2¾ million	Pensioners make up almost half of those on income support for two years or longer, followed by sick and disabled people who make up a quarter, and lone parents who make up a fifth.
6 Periods of low income (at least 2 years in 3 on a low income)	Steady	Steady	10 million	The proportion of the population in the poorest fifth range from 27% in London to 16% in the South East. In the EU, only Greece and Portugal have a higher proportion on relative low incomes than the UK.
7 The location of low income	N/A	N/A		
Children				
8 Living in workless households	Improved	Improved	2 million	Children are 30% more likely than people on average to be in a low income household. The concentration of poor children within particular primary schools is continuing to rise.
9 Living in low income households (below 60% of median income)	Steady	Improved	4 million (after housing costs)	
10 Low birth-weight babies (%)	Worsened	Worsened	N/A	25% higher rate among mothers in social classes IIIM – V than in social classes I–IIINM.
11 Accidental deaths	Improved	Improved	500 per year	1½ times the rate among children in social classes IIIM – V than in social classes I–IIINM.
12 Low attainment at school: pupils gaining no GCSE above grade D	Improved	Improved	150,000 in England and Wales	At key stage 2 (11 years old), children in schools with at least one-third of pupils on free school meals are around 25% less likely to reach level 4 than pupils in other schools.
13 Permanently excluded from school	Improved	Improved	9,500 per year	Four times the rate among black Caribbean children compared with white children.
14 Children whose parents divorce	Improved	Improved	140,000 per year	Over half the children in lone parent families are in the poorest fifth of the population compared with a fifth for children in couples with families.

Indicator	Trend — Over the medium term	Trend — Over latest year of available data	Approximate numbers affected in latest years	Variation across groups
15 Births to girls conceiving under age 16	Improved	Improved	4,000 per year	Girls in social class V are ten times as likely to become mothers in their teens as girls in social class I.
16 In young offender institutions (age 10 to 16)	Worsened	Worsened	3,000 per year in England and Wales	
Young adults				
17 Unemployed (age 16 to 24)	Improved	Improved	500,000	The unemployment rate among 18- to 24-year-olds is double that for older workers.
18 On low rates of pay (age 16 to 21)	Steady	Steady	500,000	More than half of low-paid adults work in the hotel, catering and distribution trades.
19 Not in education, training or work (age 16 to 18)	Steady	Worsened	150,000	Nearly a fifth of those not in education, training or work live independently.
20 Problem drug abuse (age 15 to 24)	Worsened	Steady	15,000 treatment episodes in six months	N/A
21 Suicide (age 15 to 24)	Improved	Improved	600 per year	Double the rate for social classes IIIM to V than for social classes I to IIINM.
22 Without a basic qualification (age 19)	Improved	Improved	200,000	N/A
23 With a criminal record (age 18 to 20)	Steady	Improved	50,000 convictions per year	Black young adults are seven times as likely to be in prison than white young adults, and ten times as likely as Asian young adults.
Adults (age 25 to retirement)				
24 Individuals wanting paid work	Improved	Improved	3¹/₂ million	Twice the rate among Black and Bangladeshi adults as the rest of the population.
25 Households without work for two years or more	Steady	Steady	2 million	Nearly a half of all lone parents do not have paid work.
26 On low rates of pay	Improved	Steady	1¹/₂ million	Low pay is much more prevalent in the distribution, hotels and catering industries than other industries.
27 Insecure at work	Steady	Steady	N/A	N/A
28 Without access to training	Steady	Steady	N/A	Three times less likely for those without qualification than for those with.
29 Premature death	Steady	Improved	N/A	Significantly worse in Scotland, the North of England and London.
30 Obesity	Worsened	Improved	20% classified as obese	1¹/₂ times more prevalent amongst women in social classes IIIM to V than in social classes I to IIINM.
31 Limiting long-standing illness or disability	Steady	Improved	3¹/₂ million	1¹/₂ times more prevalent among unskilled and junior compared with professional and managerial.
32 Mental health	Steady	Worsened	3¹/₂ million	1¹/₂ times more prevalent in the poorest two-fifths of the population compared with the richest two-fifths.

Indicator	Trend		Approximate numbers affected in latest years	Variation across groups
	Over the medium term	Over latest year of available data		
Older people				
33 No private income	Steady	Improved	1¹/₄ million	Single pensioners and pensioners aged over 75 are 1¹/₂ times more likely to be in the poorest fifth of the population than pensioner couples aged 75 and under.
34 Spending on 'essentials'	Steady	Improved	N/A	Those mainly dependent on the state pension spend 20% less on food than other pensioners.
35 Excess winter deaths	Worsened	Worsened	20,000–50,000 each year	The poorest pensioners are twice as likely to live in poorly insulated homes as the best-off pensioners.
36 Limiting long-standing illness or disability	Steady	Improved	4 million	For men, 35% higher rate among the unskilled compared with the average.
37 Anxiety (feeling unsafe out at night)	Steady	Steady	5 million	County councils and unitary authorities support far fewer pensioners in living independently at home than urban or Welsh authorities.
38 Help from social services to live at home (%)	Worsened	Worsened	N/A	
39 Without a telephone	Improved	Improved	200,000	Those without private income are three times as likely as other pensioners not to have a phone.
Communities				
40 Non-participation in civic organisations	Steady	Worsened	10 million	The poorest fifth of the population are 1¹/₂ times less likely to participate than the richest fifth.
41 Polarisation of work (%)	Steady	Steady	N/A	In two-thirds of households in social housing, the head of household is not in paid work, compared with one-third of heads of households in other tenures.
42 Spending on travel	Improved	Improved	N/A	The poorest fifth of the population spend one-quarter of what those with average incomes spend.
43 Lacking a bank or building society account	Steady	Steady	N/A	The poorest fifth of the population are 3.5 times as likely not to have an account as those with average incomes.
44 Burglaries	Improved	Improved	1¹/₄ million	Lone parent and young households are twice as likely as average to be burgled.
45 Without household insurance	Improved	Steady	N/A	Households without insurance are almost three times as likely to be burgled as those with insurance. More than half of the poorest households are uninsured compared with a fifth of those on average incomes.
46 Dissatisfaction with local area (%)	Steady	Steady	N/A	Poor households are nearly twice as likely to be dissatisfied as the average.
47 Without central heating	Improved	Improved	N/A	More prevalent in the private rented sector as in other tenures.
48 Overcrowding	Improved	Improved	500,000 households	Three times as prevalent in rented housing than in owner occupation.
49 Households in temporary accommodation	Worsened	Worsened	80,000	N/A
50 Mortgage arrears	Improved	Improved	20,000	N/A

1 Poverty and low income

Why the indicators were chosen

This chapter looks at a range of indicators of income poverty, picking up on both long-term and shorter term trends, and covering both income inequality and what is happening to the incomes of the poorest in real terms. It also provides indicators on persistent low income and on some of the geographical patterns in the distribution of people on low incomes.

In discussing income poverty, we have tried to use a variety of indicators which collectively provide a reasonably full picture of what is happening. In so doing, we have inevitably had to make choices from a wide range of possibilities. Those interested in this range of possibilities and the reasons for the particular definitions that we have used should refer to the material presented later in this chapter under the heading 'Choices in the definition of particular indicators' (page 16).

Income levels

The first indicator is the '**gap between low and median income**', comparing the incomes before housing costs of someone a tenth of the way up the income distribution with someone half-way up. The movement between these two points is a good indicator of relative poverty and social exclusion, demonstrating the extent to which the poorest are keeping up with or falling behind society's norm.

The second indicator, the '**number of individuals in households with less than 60 per cent of median income**', looks at the number of people who are living on low incomes, using a relative threshold. This threshold is used both by the EU and by the UK government when looking at trends in the numbers of people in income poverty.

Since it is also important to know the extent to which the incomes of the poorest are falling or rising in real terms, the indicator also shows the number of people below a fixed threshold that rises with inflation.

The third indicator, the '**intensity of low income**', shows what has been happening over a longer time frame, since 1979, in the numbers with less than 50 per cent, 60 per cent and 70 per cent of median income.

The fourth indicator, '**in receipt of means-tested benefit**', shows the trends in the total numbers of working age people in Britain whose incomes depend, at least in part, on one of the following benefits/tax credits: income support, jobseeker's allowance, family credit/working families tax credit and disability working allowance/disabled person's tax credit. To allow like-for-like comparisons over time, figures are presented both including and excluding the recent tax credits and the benefits that they replaced.

In each case, the second graph shows how the indicator varies between different groups of the population, demonstrating which groups are at a particularly high risk of poverty.

Income dynamics

The duration of time spent on a very low income can have a considerable effect on the deprivation of a person or family. The majority of individuals who experience persistent low income are claiming either income support (IS) or jobseeker's allowance (JSA). The first indicator in this section is the '**number of recipients claiming JSA or IS for two years or more**'.

In addition to those who spend long periods on the same very low income level, there is a substantial group whose incomes fluctuate into and out of low income. The second indicator of income dynamics is the '**number of individuals who have spells on low income in at least two years in three**'. Note that many of those whose incomes fluctuate on and off low income do not actually experience periods of above average incomes, since the fluctuations occur around the lower half of the income distribution.[1]

The final indicator is the '**location of low income**', showing how the proportion of the population who are poor varies between different regions in England. The second graph compares the proportion of the population on low income across the EU.

What the indicators show

In all cases, our indicators use the latest data available. For statistics about benefit recipients, this typically means data from 2000 or 2001. For income statistics, it means 1999/00 data.

The fact that official data on income is always between 18 and 30 months out of date is a major problem, over which we have no control. It means that any factual assessment of the success or otherwise of the Government's major initiatives (working families tax credit, minimum income guarantee, etc.) is inevitably retrospective. It is also simply not yet possible for either the Government or independent observers to say with any degree of certainty whether or not its targets for reductions in child poverty during its first term have actually been achieved or not.

It also means that any interpretation of what the indicators are showing needs to be based on a clear understanding of the precise timing of the Government's initiatives; for example, because the working families tax credit was only being introduced in October 1999, it would not have had a major impact on the 1999/00 figures. In this context, the table below summarises some of the major, relevant Government initiatives in recent years.

Timeline	Subject
November 1998	5 per cent rise in the levels of income support for recipients with children (over April 1998)
April 1999	15 per cent rise in child benefit Introduction of national minimum wage Introduction of minimum income guarantee for pensioners (but only at a rate slightly higher than the income support that it replaced)
October 1999	9 per cent rise in the levels of income support for recipients with children (over April 1999) Introduction of working families tax credit, replacing family credit Introduction of disabled person's tax credit, replacing disability working allowance
1999/00 (in practice, late 1999)	Latest data on the distribution of income
April 2000	5 per cent rise in the levels of income support for recipients with children 4 per cent rise in child benefit 5 per cent rise in the level of the minimum income guarantee Wider eligibility criteria for working families tax credit
August 2000	Latest data on numbers receiving benefits (typical)
October 2000	14 per cent rise in the levels of income support for recipients with children 3 per cent rise in the level of the national minimum wage 4 per cent rise in the level of the working families tax credit
April 2001	3 per cent rise in child benefit 20 per cent rise in the level of the minimum income guarantee 3 per cent rise in the level of the working families tax credit
October 2001	10 per cent rise in the level of the national minimum wage 5 per cent rise in the level of the working families tax credit

As of 1999/00, the number on low incomes remained at an historic high

In 1999/00, there were 13.3 million people living in households with less than 60 per cent of median income (after housing costs), compared with 13.4 million in 1998/99. This number has remained largely unchanged since the early 1990s,[2] after having doubled during the 1980s. In other words, inequalities in income between those who are poor and those who have average income remained constant during the 1990s, having vastly increased during the 1980s.

Although inequalities did not decrease during the 1990s, the real incomes of the poorest did increase slightly, by about 1 per cent per annum (£1.50 per week) in real terms. These increases are reflected in the fall in the numbers below the fixed threshold of 60 per cent of 1994/95 median income, from 13 million in 1994/95 to 10 million in 1999/00.

What appears to have happened is as follows: whilst the real incomes at the average increased substantially during the 1980s, the incomes of the poorest remained largely unchanged, leading to greater inequalities between them; in contrast, during the 1990s, the real incomes of the poorest started to increase whilst the rate of increase at the average slowed, with inequalities thus stabilising.

The patterns for the very poorest are similar, with a threefold increase in the numbers below 50 per cent of the median during the 1980s followed by little change during the 1990s. An alternative indicator of the numbers on low income, namely the numbers living in households below 50 per cent of mean income (after housing costs), also shows a similar pattern.[3]

Data from 1996 suggests that only Greece and Portugal had a greater proportion of their population on low incomes relative to the rest of the population than the UK.

More than half of all lone parents in 1999/00 lived on incomes below 60 per cent of the median, compared with 1 in 5 of other adults of working age. Nearly a fifth of the population – 10 million people – continued to experience low income at least two years in three.

Finally, there are significant geographic variations in the prevalence of low income. For example, 27 per cent of the London population are in the poorest fifth, compared with 16 per cent of those in the rest of the South East. Interestingly, as well as a high proportion of poor people, London also has a high proportion of rich people, raising questions about whether there is any scope for using more of London's substantial resources for combating local poverty.

The recent lack of change is disappointing but perhaps not surprising

1999/00 was the first year into the current government's programme for tackling low incomes, with the introduction of the national minimum wage, minimum income guarantee for pensioners, the working families tax credit, and higher levels of child benefit. The number on low incomes might therefore have been expected to drop substantially.

However, as discussed in more detail in the following chapters on children, adults and pensioners, the lack of change in 1999/00 is perhaps not surprising. The working families tax credit was only just being introduced and the minimum income guarantee for pensioners was not (when introduced) at a level which would have been sufficient to move people above the 60 per cent of median income threshold and many of those in receipt of the national minimum wage could still be below the threshold. Only the rises in income support for recipients with children and in child benefit might have been expected to have had a substantial impact on the figures.

If Government policies since 1999/00 are effective, one would expect to see a drop in the numbers on low income in future years. The lack of change in 1999/00 does, however, suggest that there is nothing about the current dynamics of the British economy which will help the Government to achieve its targets for substantial reductions in child poverty and thus any future reduction will depend on direct Government action.

Furthermore, at least one major group of those on low incomes, namely unemployed people, and particularly those without children, are not directly benefiting from the Government's current major policies. Indeed, at 20 per cent of average earnings, the levels of income support are at an historic low in recent times, down from 30 per cent in 1983.

Falling numbers of working age recipients of means-tested benefits

The total number of working age claimants of means-tested benefits and tax credits increased by 150,000 – or 4 per cent – in 2000. However, this rise was entirely due to the wider eligibility criteria for the working families tax credit and the disabled person's tax credit, in comparison with the benefits that they replaced. If these benefits and tax credits are excluded, then on a like-for-like basis, the total number of working age claimants of means-tested benefit continued to fall and by 2000 was three-quarters of the level of 1995. The number of working age long-term recipients of means-tested benefits shows a similar pattern.

Two-fifths of working age claimants have disabilities or are long-term sick, as are half of working age long-term claimants.

Choices in the definition of particular indicators

No single indicator or group of indicators can possibly capture the full complexity of income poverty in the UK. But any quantitative presentation of trends in income poverty necessarily has to restrict itself to a limited number of indicators. The challenge is to choose these indicators such that they best illustrate the essence of what has been happening. The material below discusses some of the principles that we have used in making these choices.

Note that, although they typically follow similar trends over time, the various indicators discussed below can give very different answers in terms of absolute numbers. For example:

Measure	*Number of people in households below the threshold (millions, 1999/00)*
Half of average income (after housing costs)	14.0
60 per cent of median income (after housing costs)	13.3
60 per cent of 1994/95 median income (after housing costs)	10.2
60 per cent of median income (before housing costs)	10.0
Half of median income (after housing costs)	8.7

'Moving thresholds' versus 'fixed thresholds'
It is generally accepted that poverty is concerned with a lack of possessions, or ability to do things, which are in some sense considered 'normal' or 'essential' in society.

What is considered 'normal' depends on the society in which the person lives. So, for example, a widely accepted indicator of developing countries' poverty is the numbers of people living on less than $1 per day, on the grounds that people on such incomes are literally in danger of starving to death. This threshold is often termed 'absolute income poverty'. But the use of such a threshold in the UK would obviously be completely inappropriate – no-one in the UK lives on incomes anywhere near this low and its use would imply that all people with incomes above $1 per day did not suffer from serious deprivation.

What is considered 'normal' also changes over time. Levels of income that would have been considered adequate in the UK 100 years ago would certainly not be considered to be adequate nowadays. Rather, as society becomes richer, so norms change and the levels of income and resources that are considered to be adequate rises. Unless the poorest can keep up with growth in average incomes, they will progressively become more excluded from the opportunities that the rest of society enjoys.

The conclusion is that the main indicators of low income in the UK – and thus of income poverty – should be defined in terms of thresholds which rise or fall as average incomes rise or fall. Such thresholds are often termed 'moving thresholds' or indicators of 'relative poverty'.

Principle: the main thresholds of income poverty in the UK should be defined in terms of thresholds which rise or fall as average UK incomes rise or fall.

This conclusion is generally accepted by most researchers, by the EU and by the UK government.

In normal times, when average incomes are improving slowly but steadily, the use of such thresholds is probably a good indicator of changes in the extent of relative income poverty. But if incomes should fall, they become insufficient: a fall in average incomes, even if the lowest incomes remained unchanged, would clearly not represent an improvement in the capacity of the poorest to attain what society had become accustomed to as the norm.

Furthermore, sole reliance on moving thresholds can become misleading if average incomes rise dramatically. For example, incomes in Ireland have risen sharply over the last ten years or so – including incomes at the bottom end – whilst income inequalities have remained roughly constant. Many researchers and politicians in Ireland believe that sole reliance on moving thresholds gives a misleading impression by suggesting that no progress has been made in reducing the extent of poverty.

Finally, exclusive use of any single threshold encourages a concentration of effort on those just below the threshold to the exclusion of those who are the very poorest. Thus there is a continuing need to use a variety of thresholds.

Principle: the use of fixed thresholds combined with moving thresholds can help to provide a fuller picture of what is happening to the extent of income poverty.

Indicator 2 illustrates how moving and fixed thresholds have followed different paths since 1994/95. Whilst the moving threshold has remained steady, the fixed threshold has moved downwards. In other words, the real incomes of the poorest have increased at a rate roughly equal to average incomes.

What thresholds?
The threshold of low income that has been most commonly used in the UK over the last 50 years, by both government and independent experts, is 'half average (mean) income'. The rationale for this is twofold: first, it represents a level of income which is of the same order of magnitude as independent experts' estimates of 'low, but acceptable' levels of income;[4] and, second, it is arithmetically simple and relatively easy to understand. Whilst these factors are not sufficient to qualify it as a measure of poverty or as a poverty line, they do suggest that movements in the numbers below half average income will usually provide a good indication of the way that real poverty levels are moving.

In this report, however, our primary indicator of income poverty is the numbers below *60 per cent* of *median income*, rather than *50 per cent* of *mean income*. One characteristic of the median measure, in comparison to the mean, is that it is less sensitive to changes in the incomes for groups of the population. For example, if everybody below half mean income were given enough money to bring them up to half mean then, assuming all else is equal, the mean itself would rise. By contrast, if everybody below half of the median were given enough to bring them to that threshold, the median would still remain the same. This gives the median a practical advantage in terms of setting targets and goals for the numbers below a certain threshold. Furthermore, unlike the mean, the median is unaffected by changes in the incomes of the very rich and, in our view, this makes it a better indicator of what is considered normal in contemporary society. The final reason for switching to the median this year is that the UK Government and the EU have both recently indicated their preference for using the median rather than the mean.

Like both the UK Government and the EU, our primary focus is on 60 per cent of the median rather than 50 per cent. The reason for this is that 60 per cent of the median income is roughly the same income level as 50 per cent of the mean level that we have used in previous years.

Principle: even whilst continuing to use a variety of income thresholds, 60 per cent of median income is becoming the most commonly used primary threshold.

As previously discussed, looking at a variety of thresholds potentially provides a fuller picture of what is happening. One of our indicators therefore uses 50 per cent, 60 per cent and 70 per cent of median. Similarly, our research also continues to include monitoring of the mean numbers.

Duration of low income

Some commentators argue that an exclusive focus on income at a single point in time does not provide a full picture. They point out that some people ('those at risk of poverty') can temporarily have low incomes but not be suffering serious deprivation, whilst others ('those emerging from poverty') can temporarily have higher incomes but still be suffering material deprivation.[5] Rather, they argue, an important aspect of poverty is the lack of essential goods and services which arises from prolonged periods on low income.

We are sympathetic with such arguments. In response, some of our indicators look at income over time and, in particular, the number of people who are persistently on a low income (indicators 5 and 6). Furthermore, some of the indicators in other chapters look at the number of people who lack certain essential goods and services, such as food, transport, the telephone and bank accounts.

Principle: monitoring what is happening over time, as well as at a point in time, can provide a fuller picture of what is happening to the extent of income poverty.

Note that we have not attempted to construct more complex indicators which combine lack of income and lack of essential goods and services, using surveys and statistical techniques to define what is considered 'essential'. Such indicators could not easily be constructed and updated on an annual basis from government surveys.[6]

Technical matters

Housing costs

In common with most other commentators, most of the data in this chapter is presented on an 'after housing costs' basis, which is disposable income after housing costs have been removed. The reasons for this are twofold: first, housing costs can vary considerably for people in otherwise identical circumstances (e.g. pensioners who have paid off their mortgage versus pensioners who are renting); and, second, unlike a 'before housing costs' basis, the 'after housing costs' calculations are not affected by such matters as whether housing benefit – which provides for the housing costs of many of the poorest – are considered to be income or not.

Whilst the 'after housing cost' calculations are generally agreed to be more accurate, they do have the disadvantage of making the absolute levels of income less meaningful, as people find it difficult to interpret income levels after housing costs have been removed. For this reason, those of our indicators which are in terms of absolute income levels (e.g. indicator 1) are presented on a 'before housing costs' basis.

Equivalisation

Clearly, a lone adult does not require the same income as a family of four in order to have the same standard of living. However, importantly but less obviously, economies of scale mean that the family of four does not require four times the level of income: many costs can be shared. To estimate the number of people below particular income thresholds requires that these incomes are adjusted to reflect the family grouping and thus put on a like-for-like basis. This process is called 'equivalisation'. For the scales used by the Department for Work and Pensions, for example, the income of a couple is divided by around 1.8 to put it on the same basis as a single adult, and the income of a family of two

Selected major initiatives under way

Indicators	Policy	Start date	Key department	Key delivery agency	Budget/target/comments
Indicators of low income	National minimum wage	April 1999: introduced. October 2000: uprated. October 2001: uprated.	DTI	Inland Revenue and employers	When introduced, set at £3.60 per hour for those over 22 years, unless in an exempt category or on a registered training scheme (in which case only £3.20). £3.00 per hour for those aged 18 to 21. Increases to £3.70 in October 2000 and £4.10 in October 2001 (£3.20 and £3.50 for those aged 18 to 21). To be increased to £4.20 (and £3.60) in October 2002. The Low Pay Commission estimates that the original national minimum wage affected 1.3 million jobs, potentially rising to 1.5 million after the October 2001 increases.
	Pensioners' minimum income guarantee	April 1999: introduced. April 2000: uprated. April 2001: uprated.	DWP	DWP	From April 1999: £75 a week for single pensioners and £116.60 for pensioner couples, representing increases of around £4 and £7 respectively over the levels of income support that were previously available. From April 2000: increased to £78.45 for single pensioners and £121.95 a week for pensioner couples. From April 2001: increased to £92.15 and £140.55 respectively. Under the Pensioners Credit Scheme (2003), the amounts will rise to £100 and £154 respectively. Available to anyone with an income below the threshold and with savings of no more than £12,000 (April 2001). The Government estimates that 2 million pensioners are eligible. A take-up campaign was undertaken during 2000 – 2.4m people were contacted and 110,000 claims were made. Annual budget of around £4bn (2000/01).
	Child benefit	April 1999: uprated. April 2000: uprated. April 2001: uprated.	DWP and Treasury	Benefits Agency	April 1999: up to £14.40 for eldest child (a £2.50 increase above inflation). April 2000: up to £15 for eldest child, £10 other children and £17.55 for eldest child of lone parents. April 2001: up to £15.50 for eldest child, £10.35 other children and £17.55 (unchanged from previous year) for eldest child of lone parents.
	Increase for income support recipients with children	November 1998: uprated. October 1999: uprated. April 2000: uprated.	DWP	Benefits Agency	An additional £2.50 per week in November 1998, £4.70 in October 1999, £1.10 in April 2000 and £4.35 in October 2000, with the eligibility criteria differing slightly in the different years. The April 2000 rise aligns it with 11 to 16 child credit. Estimated to benefit around 3 million children. Budget of £700 million in 2001/02.
Indicators of low income *and* **Indicators of numbers on benefit**	Working families tax credit (replacing family credit)	October 1999: introduced. October 2000: uprated. April 2001: uprated. October 2001: uprated.	Treasury and DWP	Inland Revenue and employers	When first introduced, guaranteed a weekly gross income of £200 for a family with one full time worker. No tax until £235 per week for families with one full-timer (55p taper, down from 70p under family credit). The level of the credit depends on number of children, how many hours worked (the minimum is 16 hours) and childcare costs. Guaranteed weekly income rose to £208 in October 2000, to £214 in April 2001, and to £225 in October 2001. Aims to benefit 1½ million families (twice as many as family credit). As of February 2001, 1¼ million families were claiming. The 2001 budget estimated that families on WFTC were on average £30 a week better off than they were under family credit. Provides £5bn of help each year, compared with the £3½bn of family credit.
	Disabled person's tax credit (replacing disability working allowance)	October 1999: introduced. April 2001: uprated. October 2001: uprated.	Treasury and DWP	Inland Revenue and employers	Changes broadly follow the WFTC. Originally guaranteed a weekly income of £230 for a couple with one child. Increased to £246 in April 2001 and £257 in October 2001. On introduction, the government estimated that it would double take-up to 24,000.

Gap between low and median income

Indicator
1

Disposable incomes for low income households have risen by £20 per week over the last ten years, compared with a £40 increase for the average household. Inequalities (i.e. the ratio between these two income levels) have not changed

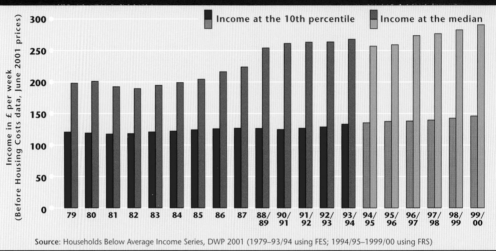

Source: Households Below Average Income Series, DWP 2001 (1979–93/94 using FES; 1994/95–1999/00 using FRS)

In 2000, income support was only 20 per cent of average earnings, compared with 22 per cent in the mid 1990s and nearly 30 per cent in the early 1980s

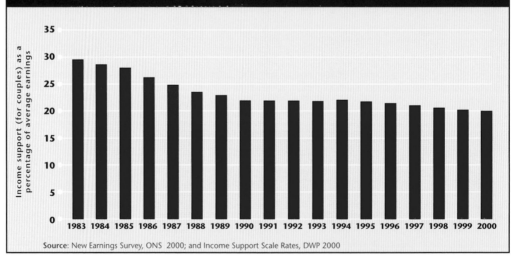

Source: New Earnings Survey, ONS 2000; and Income Support Scale Rates, DWP 2000

The first graph shows the income of individuals at different points on the income distribution: for a 'poorer' individual at the 10th percentile (i.e. 10 per cent of the population received an income below that value); and for an 'average' individual at the 50th percentile (i.e. the median).

Income is weekly disposable household income, adjusted for the size of the household, before housing costs, measured at June 2001 prices. The data source is the Family Expenditure Survey (FES) to 1993/94 and the Family Resources Survey (FRS) thereafter (shown on the graph in a different shade). The data relates to Great Britain and has been equivalised for different household compositions.

The second graph shows the value of income support for a married couple as a percentage of the average gross weekly pay of a full-time employee on adult rates.

Note that the New Earnings Survey (NES) data includes individual employees and not couples. Care should therefore be taken when comparing NES data with income support data.

*Overall adequacy of the indicator: **high**. The FES and FRS are both well-established annual government surveys, designed to be representative of the population as a whole. Note, however, that they only cover people living in private households and do not cover people in residential institutions (such as nursing homes), sleeping rough, or in bed and breakfast accommodation*

Individuals with
low income

Indicator
2

In 1990/00, 13 million people lived in low income households, largely unchanged over the previous five years. As real incomes have risen, the numbers below a fixed 1994/95 low income threshold have fallen to 10 million

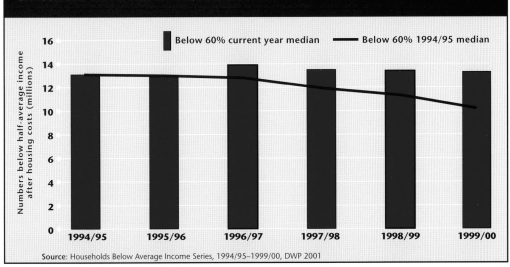

Source: Households Below Average Income Series, 1994/95–1999/00, DWP 2001

A third of those living on low incomes live in households where the head of household has some form of paid work

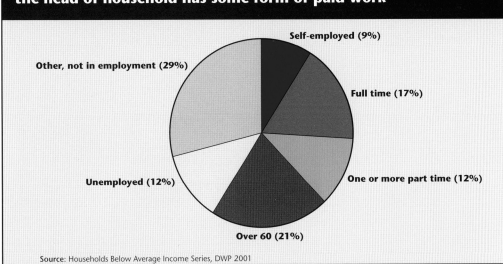

Source: Households Below Average Income Series, DWP 2001

The first graph shows the number of people below half-average income for years since 1994/95. Two measures are shown, corresponding to two different definitions of low income: 'relative' low income, i.e. half the current year average (median) income; and 'fixed' low income, i.e. half the 1994/95 average income (adjusted for price inflation).

The second graph classifies those below 'relative' half average income in 1999/00 according to the economic status of the head of household. 'Other not in employment' includes those without work who are long-term sick, or disabled, or lone parents.

Note that in previous years the measure of low income adopted was the mean. The data published this year cannot therefore be compared with that published in previous years.

Income is weekly disposable household income equivalised for household membership, before housing costs. The data source is the Family Resources Survey (FRS). The data relates to Great Britain.

Data is equivalised (adjusted) to account for variation in household size and composition. The income needs of a single person with no dependants, for example, are lower than that of a family with children. Income is divided into scales which vary according to the number of adults and the number and age of dependants in the household.

Overall adequacy of the indicator: **high.** *The FRS is a well-established annual government survey, designed to be representative of the population as a whole.*

Intensity of low income

Indicator
3

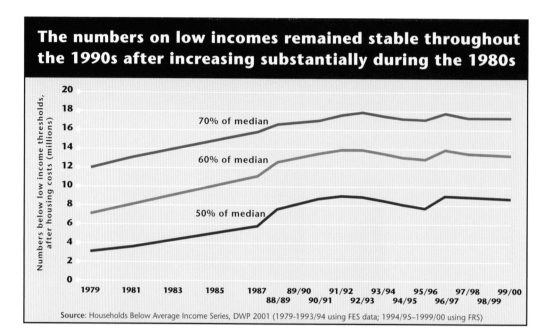

The numbers on low incomes remained stable throughout the 1990s after increasing substantially during the 1980s

Source: Households Below Average Income Series, DWP 2001 (1979-1993/94 using FES data; 1994/95–1999/00 using FRS)

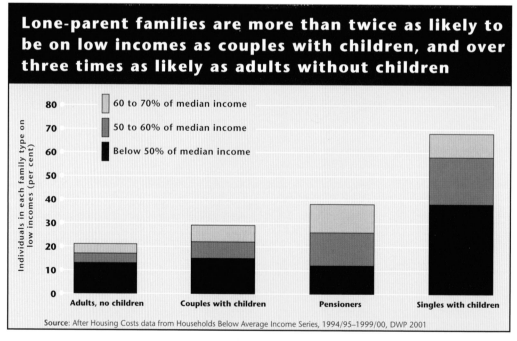

Lone-parent families are more than twice as likely to be on low incomes as couples with children, and over three times as likely as adults without children

Source: After Housing Costs data from Households Below Average Income Series, 1994/95–1999/00, DWP 2001

The first graph shows the number of people below 50 per cent, 60 per cent and 70 per cent of current year median income from 1979. Note that data for 1980, 1982–86 and 1998/90 has not been published by DWP. The graph itself therefore does not reflect actual figures for those years in question. Family Expenditure Survey (FES) data is used up to 1993/94 and Family Resources Survey (FRS) data is used from 1994/5 onwards.

Income is weekly disposable income, equivalised for household membership, after housing costs. The data relates to Great Britain. This 'after housing cost' measure of income is preferred here because the focus is exclusively on those on low income and their composition.

The second graph, using data for 1999/00, shows the percentages below each of the three thresholds for each family type. The types are: one or more adults without children; couples with children; lone adults with children; and pensioners. The data source is the FRS.

Data is equivalised (adjusted) to account for variation in household size and composition. The income needs of a single person with no dependants, for example, are lower than that of a family with children. Income is divided into scales which vary according to the number of adults and the number and age of dependants in the household.

Overall adequacy of the indicator: **high**. *The FRS and FES are both well-established annual government surveys, designed to be representative of the population as a whole. A qualification is that numbers below 50 per cent are subject to greater uncertainty, particularly when looking at different family types separately: there is some tendency for the data to under-represent young single people on low incomes and to over-represent families with children on low incomes.*

In receipt of means-tested benefit

Indicator
4

On a like-for-like basis, the number on means-tested benefits continues to fall, but only slowly

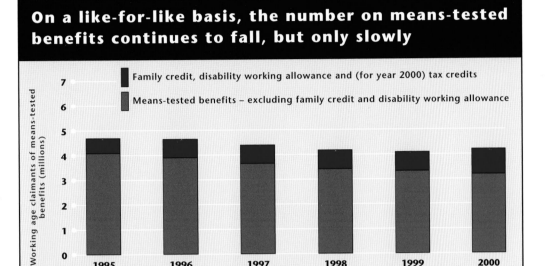

Source: Client Group Analyses, Quarterly Bulletin on Population of Working Age, DWP, August 2000
Note: In October 1999, tax credits (working families tax credit and disabled person's tax credit) replaced family credit and the disability working allowance

Sick and disabled people make up two-fifths of all working people on a means-tested benefit

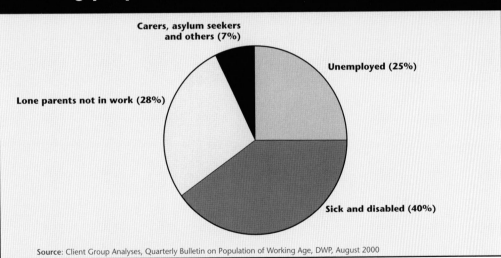

Source: Client Group Analyses, Quarterly Bulletin on Population of Working Age, DWP, August 2000

The first graph shows the total number of working age people in receipt of a means-tested benefit or (from 2000) a tax credit. In order to retain comparability over time, recipients of means-tested benefits are split between those in receipt of income support or jobseeker's allowance, and those in receipt of family credit or disability working allowance. The latter two became tax credits in October 1999 and are now known as the working families tax credit and the disabled person's tax credit respectively.

The second graph shows the relative sizes of different groups on means-tested benefits only (income support, jobseeker's allowance) for August 2000.

The data is based on information collected by the DSW for the administration of benefits and by the Inland Revenue for the administration of tax credits. For benefits, by matching data from individual samples, an estimate can be made of the number of people claiming at least one of the key benefits that are available to the population of working age. Analysis of such factors as family type and numbers of children are based only on those for whom some additional allowance of benefit is payable. The data does not include those whose incomes make them eligible, but nevertheless do not claim benefit to which they are entitled.

*Overall adequacy of the indicator: **high**. The data is thought to be very reliable and this provides an accurate count of those on benefit.*

Long-term recipients of benefit

Indicator
5

The number of long-term claimants of means-tested benefit continues to fall, but only slowly. One and a half million of those currently claiming means-tested benefits are of working age

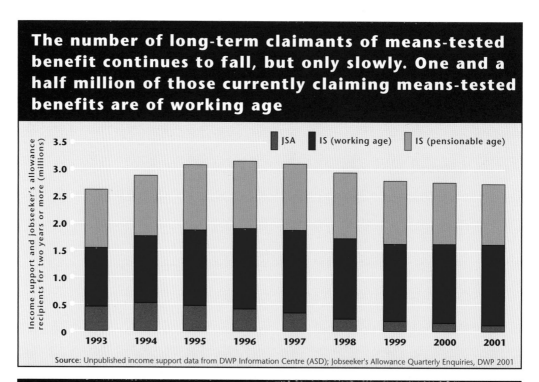

Source: Unpublished income support data from DWP Information Centre (ASD); Jobseeker's Allowance Quarterly Enquiries, DWP 2001

Pensioners make up almost half of those on income support for two years or longer, sick and disabled people make up a quarter, and lone parents make up a fifth

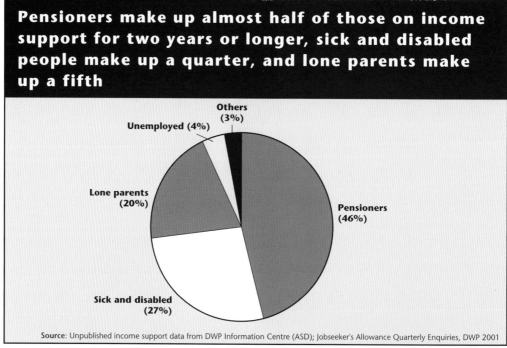

Source: Unpublished income support data from DWP Information Centre (ASD); Jobseeker's Allowance Quarterly Enquiries, DWP 2001

The first graph shows the number of people receiving either income support (IS) or jobseeker's allowance (JSA) in May of each year who had been receiving benefit for two years or more.

The second graph shows the breakdown for 2001 according to types of claimants.

*Overall adequacy of the indicator: **high***. *The data is thought to be very reliable. It is based on information collected by the DWP for the administration of benefits. By matching individual samples, a 'best estimate' can be made of the number of people claiming at least one of the key benefits that are available to the working population in each region.*

Periods of low income

Indicator
6

Nearly a fifth of the population – around 10 million people – continues to experience low income at least two years in three

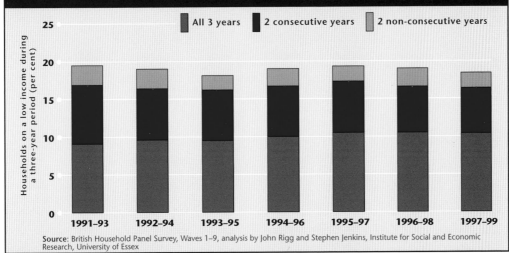

Source: British Household Panel Survey, Waves 1–9, analysis by John Rigg and Stephen Jenkins, Institute for Social and Economic Research, University of Essex

A quarter of households who spend at least some time on low income are persistently on low income

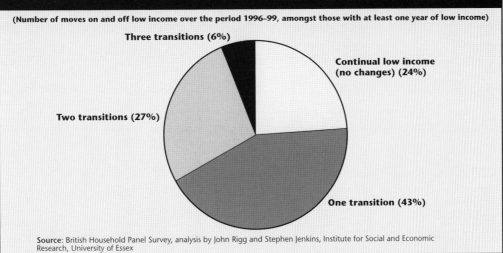

Source: British Household Panel Survey, analysis by John Rigg and Stephen Jenkins, Institute for Social and Economic Research, University of Essex

The first graph shows the number of people on low income in at least two years out of three between 1991–93 and 1997–99 (the latest years for which the analysis is available). The bars are split to show those on low income in all three years, those in two consecutive years only, and those in the first and the third year only.

The second graph takes four-year periods and classifies individuals who have some experience of low income in that period according to the number of times that they switch into or out of low income.

Income is net disposable income before housing costs, deflated and equivalised for the size of the household. Persons have low income in a given year if they are among the poorest fifth of people in that year. This group is similar to, but not the same as or directly comparable with, the people who have an income below half the average.

*Overall adequacy of the indicator: **medium**. The British Household Panel Survey is a much smaller survey than the Family Resources Survey and suffers from a loss of members over time. Care is required in interpreting the percentages since all that is recorded is the income of the individual at a point in each year, rather than continuously.*

The location of low income

Indicator
7

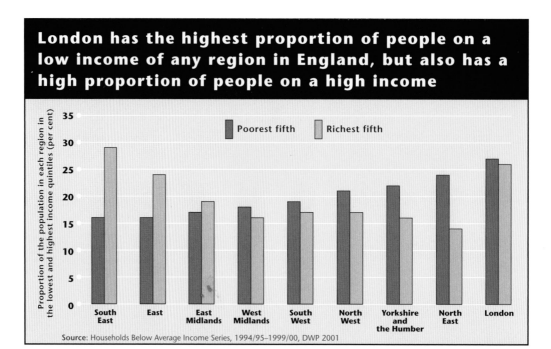

London has the highest proportion of people on a low income of any region in England, but also has a high proportion of people on a high income

Source: Households Below Average Income Series, 1994/95–1999/00, DWP 2001

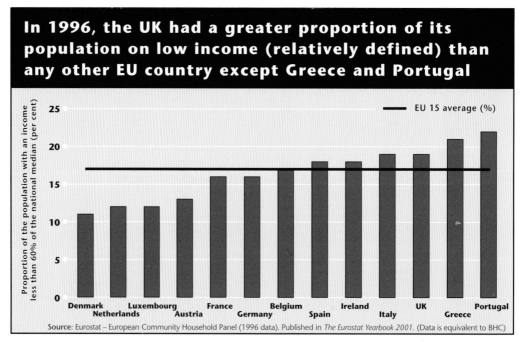

In 1996, the UK had a greater proportion of its population on low income (relatively defined) than any other EU country except Greece and Portugal

Source: Eurostat – European Community Household Panel (1996 data). Published in *The Eurostat Yearbook 2001*. (Data is equivalent to BHC)

The first graph shows the proportion of the working age population in each region claiming a key benefit, which consists of: jobseeker's allowance, incapacity benefit, severe disablement allowance, disability living allowance and income support.

The second graph shows the proportion of people in EU countries with an equivalised income that was less than 60 per cent of the median for their country in 1996.

Sixty per cent of median income is the preferred EU measure of levels of poverty. This measure is broadly similar to the percentage of the population below contemporary 60 per cent median income (17 per cent) Before Housing Costs, as published by the Households Below Average Income series, DWP. The average is for the 15 EU countries – the 13 shown plus Finland and Sweden, for which data was not available.

*Overall adequacy of the indicator: **medium**. Data for the first graph is thought to be very reliable and is based on a sample of DWP administrative data. Data for the second graph is from the European Community Household Panel, which is a smaller survey compared with the Family Resources survey (used to measure poverty in Great Britain) and suffers from a loss of members over time.*

2 Children

Why the indicators were chosen

Economic circumstances

The particular concern with children's economic circumstances arises partly from the high numbers of children in poor households and partly because of the effect of childhood poverty on the likelihood of disadvantage later in life.

Over the last two decades, a split has opened up between 'work rich' and 'work poor' households, with a large number of children in households where none of the adults have paid work. The first indicator is the **'number of children living in workless households'**.

In Britain, a greater proportion of children live in poverty than adults. The second indicator for children's economic circumstances is the **'number of children living in households with less than half-average income'**.

Health and well-being

Our first indicator of health inequalities is the **'percentage of low birth-weight babies by social class'**, chosen because it is closely correlated with poor health in the first weeks of life, with death before the age of 2 years and with ill health in later years.[1]

The second indicator is the **'number of accidental deaths amongst children aged 0 to 15 years old'**. Accidents are the commonest cause of hospital admission for children aged 5 to 15 years.[2] They are also the biggest single cause of childhood deaths, causing nearly one half of all deaths for 1- to 19-year-olds.[3]

Education

Those without qualifications are at a high risk of being unemployed or on low wages as adults.[4] More generally, success in acquiring formal qualifications bolsters self-esteem, and enhances a healthy development of self-identity. The first educational indicator is the **'numbers failing to obtain a qualification above a grade D at GCSE'**.

Permanent school exclusions have been the focus of public attention in the last few years, with the Government setting new targets to keep levels under control.[5] A high proportion of children excluded from school, particularly those at secondary level, do not return to mainstream education. The second education indicator is the **'number of children permanently excluded from school'**.[6]

Social stability

Successful child development depends in part on stable emotional and physical environments. The first indicator of social stability reflects one aspect of family stability, the **'number of children whose parents divorce'**. Family breakdown is associated with the development of mental health problems in children and young people,[7] and with lower educational attainment and employment prospects.[8]

One economically vulnerable group is girls who give birth as teenagers.[9] The second indicator of social stability is the **'number of births to girls conceiving under age 16'**.

The final indicator is the **'number of children in custodial care'**. High re-conviction rates of those aged under 17 discharged from custody[10] illustrate the heightened risks of young offenders developing criminal careers which may exclude them from mainstream society on a long-term basis.

What the indicators show
Little improvement in child poverty as of 1999/2000
Children continue to be more likely than adults to live in **low income households**. Using one of the government's preferred measures of low income – below 60 per cent of median income after housing costs – the number of children in low income households remained at around 4 million throughout the 1990s. This represents a third of all children, compared with a quarter for the population overall. Furthermore, in 1999/00, there were more children in the poorest fifth of households than in the richest two-fifths put together.[11] This is largely due to the fact that more than half of all children in lone-parent families are in the poorest fifth.

The numbers of children in households below 60 per cent of median income fell by around 300,000 between 1996/97 and 1999/00. This relatively modest reduction is perhaps not surprising – whilst child benefit was increased in April 1999, the working families tax credit was only introduced in October 1999 and, as such, did not materially affect the 1999/00 figures.[12]

The Government claims that 1.2 million children were lifted out of poverty by the end of the last parliament (using the below 60 per cent median income measure).[13] Given the fall of 300,000 between 1996/97 and 1999/00, a net reduction of 1.2 million will only have been achieved if there were further falls of 900,000 in 2000/01. Both the Government and outside observers will have to wait for the official 2000/01 figures (likely to be published in July 2002) to see if such a reduction has actually been achieved.

Achieving the Government's strategic target of eliminating child poverty by 2020 will require average net annual reductions of 200,000 throughout each of the next 20 years.

In Spring 2001, around two million children were living in **workless households**, a reduction of 500,000 since its peak in 1994. This rate of reduction does, however, compare unfavourably with the halving in unemployment over the same period. Analysis of key benefit recipients shows a similar picture: whereas the numbers of households without children in receipt of such benefits reduced by a third between 1995 and 2001, the reduction was less than a fifth for families with children.

These figures imply that achievement of the Government's strategic objective of eliminating child poverty will depend on adequate policies being in place to relieve poverty in households which remain workless as well on those work-related policies which are the focus of much of the current political debate.[14]

Continuing improvements in educational outcomes
The proportion of those finishing school **with no GCSE grades above grade D** fell by 20 per cent between 1991/92 and 1999/00.[15] There has been a 40 per cent reduction in the proportion of 11-year-olds failing to achieve level 4 or above at key stage 2 in English and maths since 1996. Whilst key stage 2 results in schools with a relatively high numbers of children on free school meals also improved by 30 per cent over the same period, they continue to be much worse than in other schools.

The number of **school exclusions** fell sharply in 1999/00, for the second successive year, and are now 30 per cent below their peak in 1996/97. There were proportionally greater falls amongst children from minority ethnic groups.

These improvements should not, however, be taken to imply that all the problems have been fully resolved. Each year, 150,000 pupils still fail to obtain any GCSEs above grade D, and 25,000 still get no grades at all. Exclusion in English schools is still four times as common for Black Caribbean pupils as for whites. Furthermore, the concentration of poor children within particular primary schools continues to increase.

To tackle these inequalities, the government has established 73 Education Action Zones, based in areas of deprivation and low educational achievement. However, its targets are expressed in overall terms (e.g. 80 per cent pass rate for English key stage 2 by 2002) and these could well be achieved whilst still leaving significant differences between the results in deprived areas and the rest of the country. Similarly, whilst the target of reducing school exclusions by a third from their 1997/98 levels by 2002 has already been achieved, significant differences between ethnic groups remain.

A mixed picture for health and social stability

The number of **accidental deaths** of children has halved over the last decade. This has contributed to the UK's position of now having the lowest rate of child deaths from injuries in the developed world, second only to Sweden, according to UNICEF.[16] But children from the manual social classes are still one-and-a-half times more likely to die in accidents than children from non-manual social classes.

The proportion of **babies who are of low birth weight** has not changed over the last five years and there are significant differences in the incidence of low birthweight babies across social classes.

The number of **births to girls conceiving before age 16** has fallen by 20 per cent since its peak in 1996. But the vast majority of these births are concentrated in the manual social classes, and the rate of teenage conception in Britain remains much higher than elsewhere in Western Europe.[17]

There continue to be small reductions in the number of **children whose parents divorce**, which have fallen by 20 per cent since their peak in 1993.

The Government has initiated a variety of policies and targets to address some of these issues. For example, there is a target to reduce accidental deaths by at least one-fifth by 2010; the Sure Start programme for children up to 4 years of age in areas of deprivation aims to reduce the incidence of low birth-weight babies by 5 per cent by 2001/02; and there is an aim of establishing a 'firm downward trend' in the rates of conception for under-16s by 2010. The targets for accidental deaths and teenage pregnancies look to be eminently achievable, although arguably unambitious. It is too early to assess the impact of the Sure Start initiative, as it only began in June 1999 and most statistics in this year's report are for 1999 or 2000.

One issue for future monitoring is whether the inequalities between social classes also diminishes, as well as the overall totals.

Finally, the numbers of children aged 10 to 16 in **young offender institutions** and secure units continue to rise, and are now more than 50 per cent higher than a decade ago. This is despite the fact that the number of children found guilty or cautioned of an indictable offence has actually fallen over the same period.

It is noteworthy that there are no government policies or targets concerned with reducing the number of children in custody.

Selected major initiatives under way

Indicators	Policy	Start date	Key department	Key delivery agency	Budget/target/comments
8 **Children in workless households** *and* 9 **Children in low income households**	Working families tax credit (WFTC)	October 1999: introduced. October 2000: uprated. April 2001: uprated. October 2001: uprated.	Treasury and DWP	Inland Revenue and employers	When initially introduced, guaranteed a weekly gross income of £200 for a family with one full-time worker. No tax until £235 per week for families with one full-timer (55p taper, down from 70p under family credit). The level of the credit depends on number of children, how many hours worked (the minimum is 16 hours) and childcare costs. Minimum income guarantee rose to £208 in October 2000, to £214 in April 2001, and to £225 in October 2001. Aims to benefit 1½ million families (twice as many as family credit). As of February 2001, 1¼ million families were claiming. The 2001 budget estimated that families on WFTC were on average £30 a week better off than they were under family credit. Provides £5bn of help each year, compared to the £3½ bn under family credit.
	Childcare allowance (part of WFTC)	October 1999: introduced. April 2001: uprated.	Treasury and DWP	Inland Revenue and employers	Part of a wider childcare package. October 1999: up to 70 per cent of childcare costs for working parents, up to a limit of £100 for one child and £150 for two or more children. April 2001: limits raised to £135 for one child and £200 for two or more children. Since its introduction, around 90,000 families have claimed
	Children's tax credit (CTC, part of WFTC)	April 2001: introduced (replaces married couples' allowance).	Treasury and DWP	Inland Revenue	In 1999/00 Married Couple's Allowance was £197. This was replaced in 2000/01 by the CTC with a credit worth up to £520. This rises to £1,040 for newborns. Expected to reach 5 million low income families with children under age 16. Inland Revenue estimate an expenditure of £2 billion for 2001/02, with 4.5 to 5 million claimants. Will become part of the integrated child credit in 2003.
	National Childcare Strategy	May 1998: introduced.	DfES	Local authorities	Aims to create up to 1 million accessible and affordable childcare places by March 2004. By December 2004, aims to provide a childcare place in the most disadvantaged areas for every lone parent entering employment. Budget of £66m in 2000/01, rising to £200m in 2003/04.
9 **Children in low income households**	Increases for income support recipients with children	November 1998: uprated. October 1999: uprated. April 2000: uprated. October 2000: uprated. April 2001: uprated.	DWP	Benefits Agency	An additional £2.50 per week in November 1998, £4.70 in October 1999, £1.10 in April 2000 and £4.35 in April 2001, with the eligibility criteria changing slightly from April 2000. The April 2000 rise aligns it with 11 to 16 child credit. Estimated to benefit around 3 million children. Budget of £700 million in 2001/02.
	Increases in child benefit	April 1999: uprated. April 2000: uprated. April 2001: uprated.	Treasury and DWP	Benefits Agency	April 1999: up to £14.40 for eldest child (a £2.50 increase above inflation). April 2000: up to £15 for eldest child, £10 other children and £17.55 for eldest child of lone parents. April 2001: up to £15.50 for eldest child, £10.35 other children and £17.55 for eldest child of lone parents (unchanged from 2000).

Indicators	Policy	Start date	Key department	Key delivery agency	Budget/target/comments
10 Low birth-weight babies and **11 Accidental deaths**	Sure Start for children aged 0 to 4 and their families in selected areas	June 1999: introduced.	DH, DfES, Treasury, DTLR	Local authorities, voluntary sector, NHS, government and regional offices	250 Sure Start schemes to be set up by March 2002, and 500 by 2004. By 2004, aims to be reaching one-third of children under age 4 living in poverty. A variety of targets by 2002: a 10 per cent reduction in children being re-registered on child protection registers; a 5 per cent reduction in low birth-weight babies; a 10 per cent reduction in children admitted to accident and emergency units during their first year of life; and at least 90 per cent of children to have normal speech and language development at 18 months and at 3 years £450m for 1999/00 to 2001/02, and a further £580m for the period to 2004.
	Sure Start maternity grant	March 2000: introduced (replacing maternity payment scheme). Autumn 2000 – uprated	DWP	Benefits Agency	Grants for parents who provide evidence that health advice has been received from a professional and who are in receipt of qualifying benefits. Initial rate was £200; increased to £300 in Autumn 2000. A further increase to £500 is expected in April 2002. The 2002 increase is expected to benefit an additional 215,000 low income families.
12 Low attainment at school	Education Action Zones	Successive rounds from 1998. January 1999: the first 25 zones. Early 2000: a further 48 zones.	DfES	School-led local partnerships	Around £1m per zone per year.
	National Literacy and Numeracy Strategies and summer schools	Literacy hour and numeracy period from September 1998.	DfES	Schools	2,300 summer schools operative in 2000, of which 1,800 were devoted to literacy and numeracy. By 2002: 80 per cent of 11-year-olds to be at level 4 at key stage 2 in English, and 75 per cent in maths. £240m over three years (+ £16m for summer schools).
13 School exclusion	Tackling truancy and exclusion in schools	April 1998: new powers for police. September 1999: LEAs set new targets for schools.	DfES and Home Office	Schools, LEAs and police	By 2002: to reduce the number of exclusions and time lost through truancy by a third from their 1997/98 level. £500m over 1999/2002.
15 Teenage pregnancy	Measures to tackle teenage pregnancy	1999	DH	Schools, clinics, social services, etc.	By 2010: to halve the conception rates amongst under-18s in England and to establish a firm downward trend for under-16s. £760m for 1999 to 2002.

Living in workless households

Indicator
8

Around 2 million children live in workless households. Although this has been slowly falling since 1994, it is still above the level in 1990

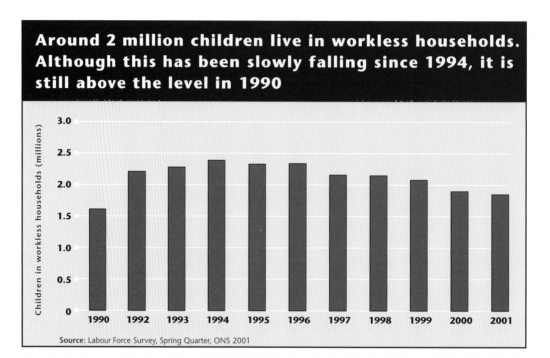

Source: Labour Force Survey, Spring Quarter, ONS 2001

Whilst there has been a sharp fall in the number of benefit claimants of working age without children, the number of claimants with children has remained largely unchanged

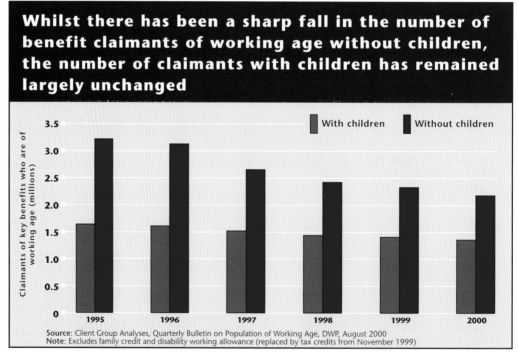

Source: Client Group Analyses, Quarterly Bulletin on Population of Working Age, DWP, August 2000
Note: Excludes family credit and disability working allowance (replaced by tax credits from November 1999)

The first graph shows the number of dependent children living in households in which none of the working age adults have paid employment. Dependent children are those aged less than 16 years. Working age households are those with at least one person of working age. Households made up of students and those in which the head of household is retired are excluded. The graph is based on the Labour Force Survey (LFS). The data covers the United Kingdom.

The second graph shows those in receipt of a key benefit (income support, job seeker's allowance, incapacity benefit or severe disablement allowance) in August of each year split by those with and without dependent children. Note that the graph omits people in receipt of family credit and disability working allowance, both of which were replaced by tax credits from October 1999.

Overall adequacy of the indicator: **high**. *The LFS is a well-established, quarterly government survey, designed to be representative of the population as a whole. Data for the second graph is considered to provide a reliable and an accurate count of those claiming the relevant benefits.*

Living in households with below half-average income

Indicator
9

Despite a modest decline over the previous three years, 4 million children still lived in low income households in 1999/00. Children are more likely than adults to live in low income households

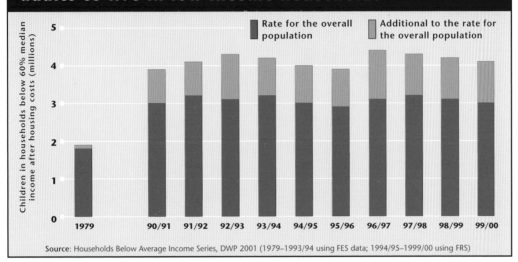

Source: Households Below Average Income Series, DWP 2001 (1979–1993/94 using FES data; 1994/95–1999/00 using FRS)

The concentration of poor children within particular primary schools continues to increase

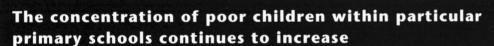
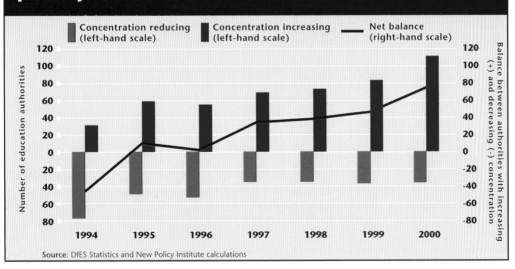

Source: DfES Statistics and New Policy Institute calculations

The first graph shows the number of children living in households below half-average income. The bar is split to show the extent to which children are at a higher risk than adults of being in households below half-average income.

Income is weekly disposable household income equivalised for household membership, after housing costs. The source is the Family Expenditure Survey to 1993/94 and the Family Resources Survey thereafter. Data is equivalised (adjusted) to account for variation in household size and composition. The income needs of a single person with no dependants, for example, are lower than that of a family with children. Income is divided into scales which vary according to the number of adults and the number and age of dependants in the household.

The second graph is a proxy for the extent to which poorer children are becoming more or less concentrated in particular areas. Using data from English local education authorities, on the proportions of children in each school entitled to free school meals, it is based on a measure of the extent to which the proportions vary between schools and within an authority.

*Overall adequacy of the indicator: **high**. The FES and FRS are well-established government surveys, designed to be representative of the population as a whole. The second graph, based on own calculations, can be regarded as **medium**.*

Low birth-weight babies

Indicator
10

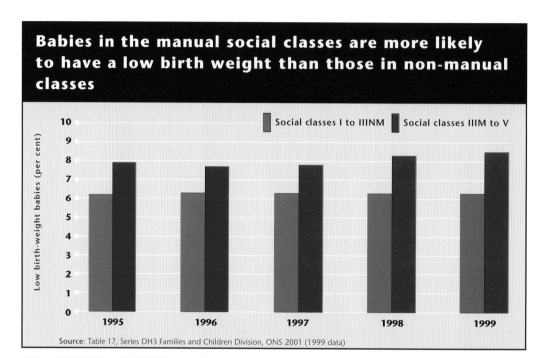

Babies in the manual social classes are more likely to have a low birth weight than those in non-manual classes

Source: Table 17, Series DH3 Families and Children Division, ONS 2001 (1999 data)

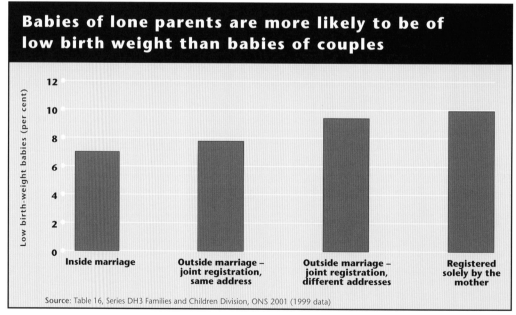

Babies of lone parents are more likely to be of low birth weight than babies of couples

Source: Table 16, Series DH3 Families and Children Division, ONS 2001 (1999 data)

The first graph shows the percentage of babies born each year who are defined as having a low birth weight, i.e. less than 2^1/$_2$ kilograms (5^1/$_2$ lbs). The percentages are shown separately for babies whose fathers are in social classes I to IIINM and IIIM to V. The data for live births is a 10 per cent sample coded to father's occupation, and excludes sole registration by mothers.

The second graph shows these percentages for 1999 according to the parents' marital status at the time of the registration of birth. The data is a 100 per cent count of live births.

The data relates to England and Wales.

*Overall adequacy of the indicator: **limited**. The data itself is large and reputable, but classification by the social class of the father may be problematic since those where no details are known about the father are not included at all. There are also problems relating to the reliability of the time series.*

Accidental deaths

Indicator
11

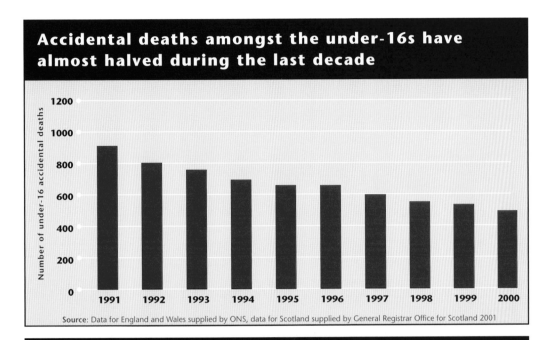

Accidental deaths amongst the under-16s have almost halved during the last decade

Number of under-16 accidental deaths

Source: Data for England and Wales supplied by ONS, data for Scotland supplied by General Registrar Office for Scotland 2001

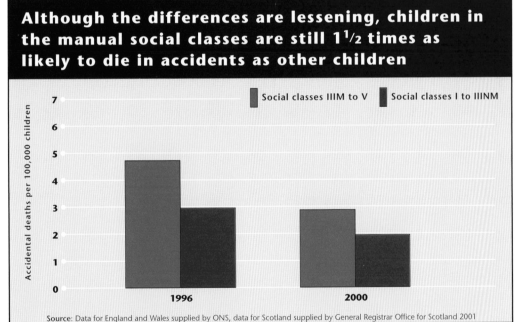

Although the differences are lessening, children in the manual social classes are still 1½ times as likely to die in accidents as other children

Accidental deaths per 100,000 children

Social classes IIIM to V   Social classes I to IIINM

Source: Data for England and Wales supplied by ONS, data for Scotland supplied by General Registrar Office for Scotland 2001

The first graph shows the annual number of deaths due to external causes among those under 16.

The second graph shows the relative likelihood of such deaths split by social classes I to IIINM and IIIM to V using the latest year's data.

'Accidental deaths' encompasses all forms of accidental death, including traffic accidents, poisoning, falls and drowning as well as suicides and homicides. Note that the method used to record mortality in Scotland was revised in 2000 (to ICD10) and that this may slightly affect data continuity.

The data relates to Great Britain.

*Overall adequacy of the indicator: **medium**. An important qualification to the split by social class is that over a third of such deaths in England and Wales are unclassified by social class, due either to a lack of information or because no socio-economic class can be attributed.*

Low attainment at school

Indicator
12

The number of 15-year-olds with no grades above a D continues to fall, but this still represents 25 per cent of all 15-year-olds (150,000 pupils). Four per cent (25,000) got no grades at all

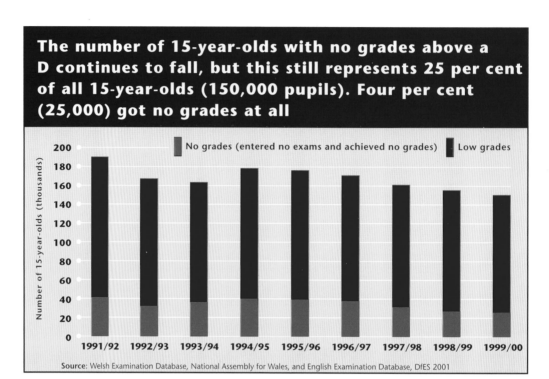

Source: Welsh Examination Database, National Assembly for Wales, and English Examination Database, DfES 2001

11-year-old pupils in schools with high numbers on free school meals do worse in English and maths than pupils in other schools

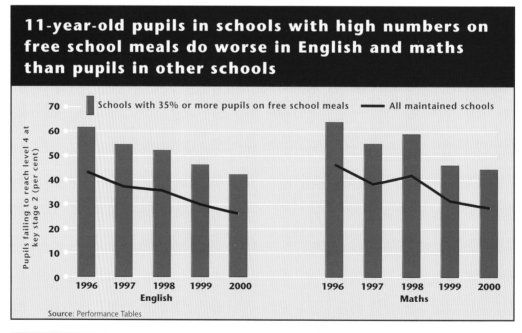

Source: Performance Tables

The first graph shows the number of 15-year-old school students (defined as pupils aged 15 at 31 August) failing to obtain at least one GCSE at grade C or above in England and Wales. The numbers are split between those who obtain no GCSE grade at all, either because they don't enter for exams or achieve no passes, and those who do obtain grades but none higher than D.

The second graph compares the percentage of children failing to reach level 4 at key stage 2 (11 years old) in schools which have at least 35 per cent of pupils on free school meals, with all maintained mainstream schools. The graph shows maths and English separately and shows changes over time. The data is for English schools only.

*Overall adequacy of the indicator: **medium**. While the data itself is sound enough, the choice of the particular level of exam success is a matter of judgement.*

Permanently excluded
from school

The number of permanent exclusions has fallen sharply over the last two years but is still three times the number of a decade ago

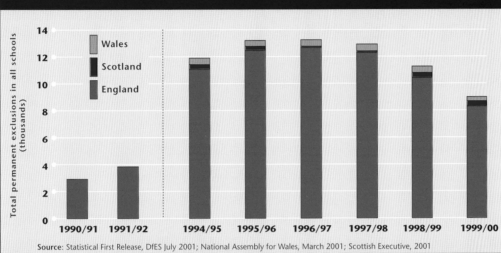

Source: Statistical First Release, DfES July 2001; National Assembly for Wales, March 2001; Scottish Executive, 2001

Although the rate of permanent exclusions of black pupils has dropped substantially over the last two years, they are still much more likely to be excluded than white pupils

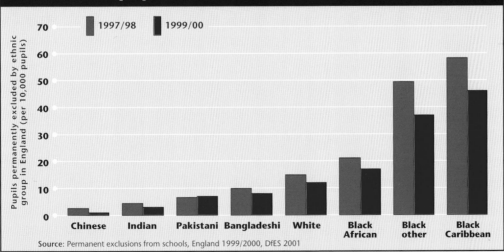

Source: Permanent exclusions from schools, England 1999/2000, DfES 2001

The first graph shows the number of pupils permanently excluded from primary and secondary schools between 1990/91 and 1999/00. Data for Scotland (referred to as 'removals from register') and Wales is shown for 1994/95 to 1999/00 only.

In Scotland, data on removals from register was collected from local authorities via a new survey from 1998/99. Previously, this information had been collected from individual schools. Data from 1994/95 to 1997/98 is therefore not strictly comparable with the new figures.

The second graph shows the rate of exclusion for children from different ethnic backgrounds in 1997/98 and 1999/00. The data relates to England only.

*Overall adequacy of the indicator: **medium**. Data prior to 1994/95 was collected on a voluntary basis and the rise in the early 1990s may in part be due to this change in the method of collection. For Scotland, data was collected on the basis of a consistent definition only from 1998/99 onwards. Exclusions are also susceptible to administrative procedures; for example, these officially recorded numbers may well under-represent the true number of exclusions if parents are persuaded to withdraw their child rather than leave the school to exclude them.*

Children whose parents divorce

Indicator
14

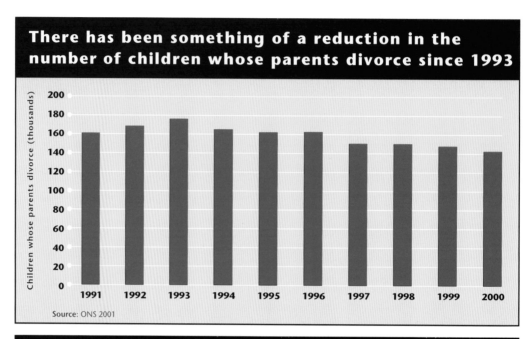

There has been something of a reduction in the number of children whose parents divorce since 1993

Source: ONS 2001

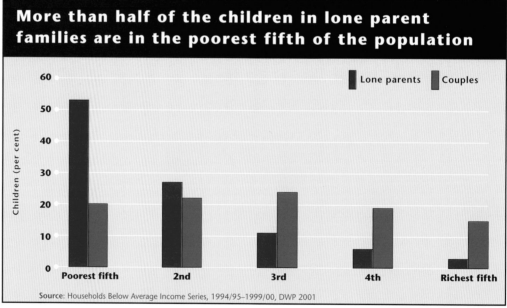

More than half of the children in lone parent families are in the poorest fifth of the population

Source: Households Below Average Income Series, 1994/95–1999/00, DWP 2001

The first graph shows the number of children under age 16 in all households whose parents divorce in the year in question. The data is for England and Wales only. In previous years we included Scottish statistics, but the Scottish Executive has recently discontinued publishing divorce statistics.

Data refers to children of the family. This includes children born to the couple divorcing, those born outside marriage, children of previous marriages and adopted children – provided that they were treated by both parents as children of the family.

The second graph shows the distribution of children across the income quintiles in 1999/00, split by whether they are living in couple or lone-parent households. The data comes from the Family Resources Survey (FRS) and relates to Great Britain.

*Overall adequacy of the indicator: **limited**. While there are few problems with the data itself (although the lack of any recent information on divorce rates by socio-economic status is clearly limiting), interpretation of movements in the indicator could be complicated by any legislative changes which make divorce either much easier or much harder. Furthermore, many children whose parents split up are not captured by this indicator.*

Births to girls conceiving under age 16

Indicator
15

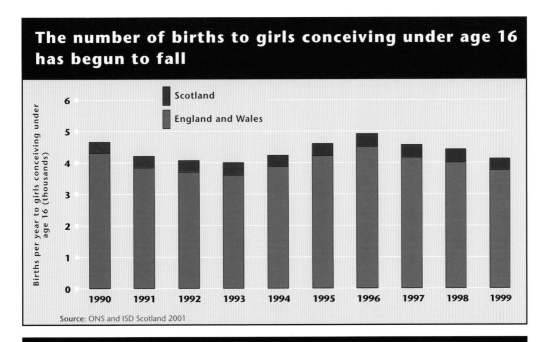

The number of births to girls conceiving under age 16 has begun to fall

Births per year to girls conceiving under age 16 (thousands)

Scotland

England and Wales

1990 1991 1992 1993 1994 1995 1996 1997 1998 1999

Source: ONS and ISD Scotland 2001

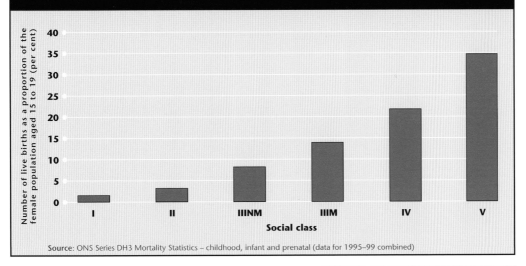

Girls whose partners are in the manual social classes are much more likely to become mothers under the age of 20 than girls whose partners are in the non-manual classes

Number of live births as a proportion of the female population aged 15 to 19 (per cent)

I   II   IIINM   IIIM   IV   V

Social class

Source: ONS Series DH3 Mortality Statistics – childhood, infant and prenatal (data for 1995–99 combined)

The first graph shows the number of births per year to girls under the age of 16. English and Welsh conceptions leading to births are counted during the actual year of conception, whilst Scottish conceptions are counted after the birth of the child, which is commonly in the calendar year following conception.

The second graph shows the distribution of live births as a proportion of the female population across the social classes, combining five years' data from 1995 to 1999. It is based on births to girls under the age of 20 by the social class of the father of the baby. The female population by social class has been estimated by allocating girls aged 14 to 19 into social classes of persons aged 0 to 15, according to 1991 census figures.

*Overall adequacy of the indicator: **medium**. The collection of these conception and births statistics is an established process. Note that the second graph leaves out around 40 per cent of live births because either social class data is not available, or because they were sole registrations and therefore details of the father's social class could not be recorded.*

In young offender institutions

Indicator
16

The number of children aged 10 to 16 who are in custody continues to rise

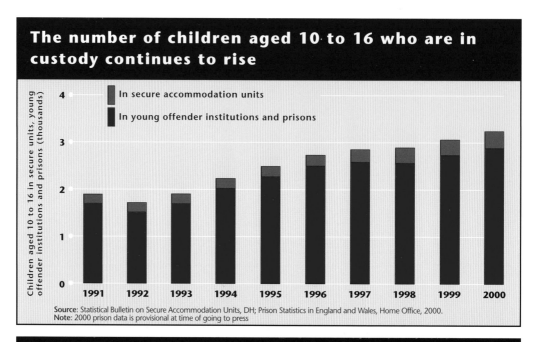

In secure accommodation units

In young offender institutions and prisons

Source: Statistical Bulletin on Secure Accommodation Units, DH; Prison Statistics in England and Wales, Home Office, 2000.
Note: 2000 prison data is provisional at time of going to press

The number of children aged 10 to 17 in England and Wales found guilty of or cautioned for indictable offences has fallen by a fifth over the last decade

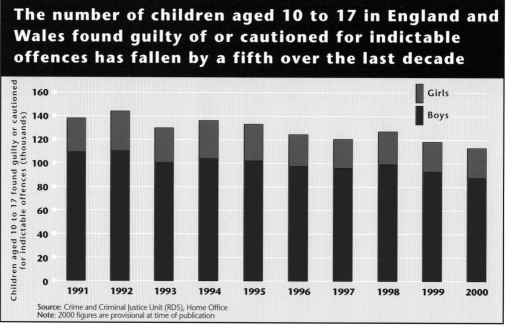

Girls

Boys

Source: Crime and Criminal Justice Unit (RDS), Home Office
Note: 2000 figures are provisional at time of publication

The first graph shows the number of children aged 10 to 16 held in young offender institutions, prison or local authority secure accommodation units. The data relates to England and Wales (note that data for Wales is from 1997 onwards only). Also, since 1993, 14-year-olds have not been held in young offender institutions.

The data for secure accommodation units measures all held on 31st March of each year. In previous years, our reports have measured admissions but the Department of Health has now discontinued collecting such data.

The second graph shows the number of children between the ages of 10 and 17 who were either cautioned for or convicted of an indictable offence. Figures for 2000 are provisional at the time of publication. The data relates to England and Wales.

The figures in the two graphs reflect police-identified crime and police practice, and should not be taken as estimates of the extent of crime carried out by children.

Overall adequacy of the indicator: **medium**. *The cautions are formal cautions only, including reprimands and final warnings introduced under the Crime and Disorder Act 1998 (from September 1998) in seven pilot areas. Informal cautions are not recorded in the statistics but, according to 1995 Home Office Criminal Statistics, rates of informal cautioning have increased in recent years.*

3 Young adults

Why the indicators were chosen

This chapter concerns young adults aged 16 to 24. This age group has often been ignored, with much of the literature, for example that on health, focusing on either children or adults.[1] In part, this is because it is widely believed that young adults are healthy and resilient. But the transition from childhood to adulthood is a critical life stage and, as with children, the well-being of this age group is an important determinant of health and well-being later in life.

Economic circumstances

There is a great diversity of economic circumstances among young adults. Some, especially students, remain dependent on their parents well into their early 20s, while others become parents themselves in their late teens. Whereas the well-paid young man or woman with few commitments can have a large part of their income available for discretionary expenditure, many of those who are not in education, training or work are effectively excluded from all the usual sources of income.

The unemployment rate among young adults is significantly higher than for adults over 25. As with other age groups, unemployment for young people is a major cause of low income and deprivation. The first indicator is the '**number of people aged under 25 who are unemployed**'.

Low wages disproportionately affect young adults and the second indicator is the '**number of 16- to 24-year-olds on low rates of pay**', where low pay is defined as half of male median hourly pay.

Young adults aged 16 and 17 have been one of the groups most affected by changes in the benefit system in the last decade. Most notably, their entitlement to income support was withdrawn in September 1988 and, for those aged 18 to 24, a reduced rate of income support is payable.

A particularly vulnerable group are those who have fallen through all the safety nets and are not employed, in training or in education. The third economic indicator is the '**number of 16- to 18-year-olds not in education, training or employment**', with the indicator showing separately those that are living independently and those living with family members.

Health and well-being

The indicators selected in this section reflect two areas – misuse of drugs and suicide rates – where recent trends have caused considerable concern, and where reported rates stand out when compared internationally.[2]

The first indicator is the '**number of young adults aged 15 to 24 starting drug treatment episodes**'. Apart from the serious health consequences that can arise from drug addiction, drug addicts are at increased risk of suicide and of developing mental health difficulties.[3] Whilst there are problems with this indicator, especially the fact that it will in part reflect the availability of agencies to help with the problem, it is the best statistic available for tracking what appear to have been sharply growing numbers of one very vulnerable group.

The second indicator is the '**suicide rate amongst 15- to 24-year-olds**'. Suicide is the second most common cause of death among young men after accidents. What makes suicide an important issue for this report is the connection between suicide and socio-economic conditions.

Barriers to work

The first barrier to work concerns lack of educational qualifications and the indicator adopted is the '**number of 19-year-olds who do not have at least an NVQ Level 2 or equivalent**'. The inclusion of this subject continues one of the core themes of the chapter on children – namely, that education is an important element in reducing the intergenerational transmission of disadvantage.

The second barrier to work concerns criminality among young adults, with the indicator being the '**number of 18- to 20-year-olds convicted of an indictable offence**'. As well as employer discrimination, the barriers which face ex-offenders include low levels of skills and qualifications, poor self-esteem, and behavioural and health problems which can reduce their chances of securing a job.[4] Furthermore, unemployment may itself increase the chances of criminality.

What the indicators show
Large numbers remain economically vulnerable
The number of young adults aged 16 to 24 who are unemployed (according to the ILO definition) continues to fall and now stands at around 1/2 million, down from 1 million in 1993. However, at 10 per cent, the unemployment rate amongst those aged 18 to 24 is still more than twice that for older workers and this gap has widened somewhat in recent years.[5]

The Government's New Deal for 18- to 24-year-olds aims to reduce the claimant count by 250,000 between 1998 and 2002. It is interesting to note that, whilst this target has apparently already been achieved, the level of unemployment measured by the ILO (which is a wider measure) has fallen by less than 100,000 over the period. Furthermore, whilst the New Deal programme has now been made permanent, the original targets have not been updated and it is not clear whether the Government views the remaining numbers of unemployed young adults as a priority group.

The Government's other major initiative has been the introduction of the national minimum wage. When first introduced in April 1999, levels were set at £3.00 per hour for those aged 18 to 21 and £3.60 per hour for those aged 22 and above, rising in 2000 to £3.20 and £3.70 respectively.

Unfortunately, official data on the prevalence of low pay is now only available for the 18 to 21 age group, and not for the 16 to 24 age group that is the focus of this chapter.[6] This data suggests that, since the introduction of the minimum wage, the number of employees aged 18 to 21 who are paid less than £3 per hour fell from 120,000 in 1998 to 50,000 in 2000.[7] In contrast, the number earning below half male median earnings – a higher threshold but still a low rate of pay – do not appear to have decreased substaintially over the period. In other words, it appears that low pay remains a major problem among young adults which the minimum wage has not yet fully resolved.

Interestingly, the numbers in the 18 to 21 age group who are paid less than the 'adult' minimum wage fell from around 400,000 in 1998 to 200,000 in 2000. This implies that the minimum wage rate for those aged 22 and over is also having an effect on pay for those aged under 22, perhaps by establishing a 'rate for the job'.

Finally, there continue to be around 150,000 young adults aged 16 to 18 at any point in time who are not in education, training or work. This is nearly 10 per cent of the age group.

Some improvement in qualifications and training, but not at the bottom end
The Government's strategy for those in their late teens is mainly to encourage full-time training or education as far as possible, rather than employment.

Around 180,000 19-year-olds – nearly a quarter of the age group – currently lack a basic qualification (NVQ2 or equivalent). Whilst this is down from a third since 1995, this rate of reduction is less than would be required to reach the Government's target of 15 per cent by 2002.

Furthermore, it is not clear that general improvements in qualification levels and employment in this age group also reflect an improved situation for the most disadvantaged. In particular, the proportion of 19-year-olds without any qualifications at all has not fallen in the last five years and, at around 60,000, is currently 8 per cent of the age group.

The suggestion that there is a continuing and substantial minority of young adults who are particularly vulnerable is supported by the observation that there are around 60,000 18- to 20-year-olds who received a criminal record in 2000, largely unchanged from five years previously. Men are seven times as likely to have a criminal record as women, and young black people are seven times as likely to be in prison as young white people.

A mixed picture on the trends in severe ill-health

The number of suicides amongst 15- to 24-year-olds in England and Wales has been declining since 1997, and the Government's target to reduce suicide rates by 20 per cent of the 1997 rate by 2010 already appears to have been achieved for young adults.

However, there have been no such decreases in Scotland where suicide rates now appear to be around three times higher than in England and Wales. Young men are still four times as likely as young women to take their lives, and young men in the manual social classes are still twice as likely to commit suicide as those in the non-manual classes.

Around 30,000 young people aged 15 to 24 start treatment for problem drug use each year, double the levels of the early 1990s. It is unclear whether these increases reflect increasing drug usage or an increasing inclination of drug misusers to seek treatment.

Two-thirds of the treatments are for heroin addiction. The Government's anti-drugs strategy aims to cut heroin and crack cocaine use by a quarter by 2005, and by a half by 2008. As indicated above, measuring the extent to which these targets are actually being achieved is somewhat problematic.

Selected major initiatives under way

Indicators	Policy	Start date	Key department	Key delivery agency	Budget/target/comments
17 Unemployment	New Deal for 18- to 24-year-olds	April 1998: introduced. April 2001: made permanent.	DfES/DWP	Employment service	Aims to reduce the claimant count by 250,000 between 1998 and 2002. Government figures are that 275,000 young people moved into employment between April 1998 and December 2000. Budgets of £200m in 1998/99, £310m in 1999/00, £400m 2000/01, £350m in 2001/02, £280m in 2002/03, and £280m in 2003/04. Additional DfES/DWP allocation of £685m in each year between 1998–2004, giving a total budget of £2.6bn by 2004.
18 On low rates of pay	National minimum wage	April 1999: introduced. October 2000: uprated. October 2001: uprated. October 2002: to be uprated.	DTI	Inland Revenue and employers	When introduced, set at £3.00 per hour for those aged 18 to 21 and £3.60 per hour for those over 22 (unless in an exempt category or on a registered training scheme, in which case only £3.20). Increases in the rate for those aged 18 to 21 to £3.20 in June 2000, £3.50 in October 2001, and £3.60 in October 2002. Increases in rate for those over 22 to £3.70 in October 2000, £4.10 in October 2001 and £4.20 in October 2002.
19 Not in education, training or work *and* 22 Without a basic qualification	Improving participation and attainment of 14- to 19-year-olds	December 1997: introduced. September 2000: widened.	DfES	Careers service	By 2002, 85 per cent of 19-year-olds with at least NVQ level 2; 50 per cent of 16-year-olds with five high grade GCSEs, and 95 per cent with at least one GCSE. By 2004, 92 per cent of 16-year-olds with five or more GCSE grades at A* to G or equivalent, including English and maths. More vocational qualifications introduced at key stage 4 in September 2000.
	Education Maintenance Allowance	September 1999: introduced. September 2000: extended.	DfES	LEAs, schools, colleges, careers service	Funding of up to £40 per week to those who stay in education, with additional retention and achievement bonuses. An initial budget of £100m for three years, increased by £93m in 2000/01. Budget for 2001/02 around 160m, but not yet confirmed.
	Connexions	April 2000: pilots. April 2001: phased launch. 2003: should cover all of England.	A range of departments: DfES, DWP, DCMS, HO,Cabinet Office, DTLR and DH.	National Unit for Connexions Service	A universal service providing advice, guidance and support for 13- to 19-year-olds, in particular to connect and reconnect with learning. Brings together new and existing services to a coherent whole. Various targets involving education, care, drugs, offending and teenage pregnancy. A budget of £320m in 2001/02, covering both Connexions and the careers service (£110m for Connexions). A provision budget of £420m for 2002/03.

Indicators	Policy	Start date	Key department	Key delivery agency	Budget/target/comments
20 Problem drug use	UK Anti-Drugs Strategy	1998	Cabinet Office, HO, DH	Drug Action Teams	A variety of targets. (1) Amongst under-25s, to reduce heroin and crack use by 25 per cent in five years and by 50 per cent in ten years. (2) To reduce repeat offending by drug misusers by 25 per cent by 2005, and by 50 per cent by 2008. (3) To increase participation of problem drug misusers, including prisoners, in drug treatment programmes by 66 per cent by 2005 and by 100 per cent by 2008. (4) To reduce availability of Class A drugs by 25 per cent by 2005 and by 50 per cent by 2008. A budget of £3.5bn for 2000 to 2004.
21 Suicide	Measures to tackle suicide rates	1998	DH	NHS	Aims to reduce suicides by 20 per cent of 1997 rate by 2010. Incorporated into both Saving Lives – *Our Healthier Nation* (Department of Health 1998), and *Modernising Mental Health* (Department of Health 1998)

Unemployment

Indicator
17

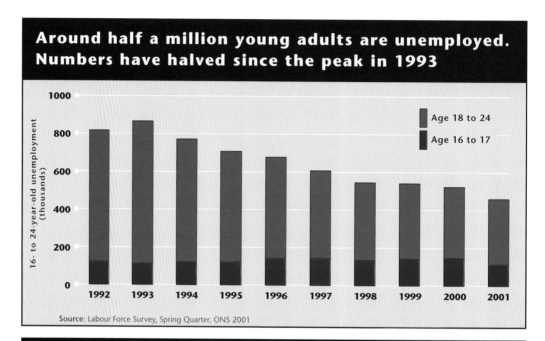

**Around half a million young adults are unemployed.
Numbers have halved since the peak in 1993**

Source: Labour Force Survey, Spring Quarter, ONS 2001

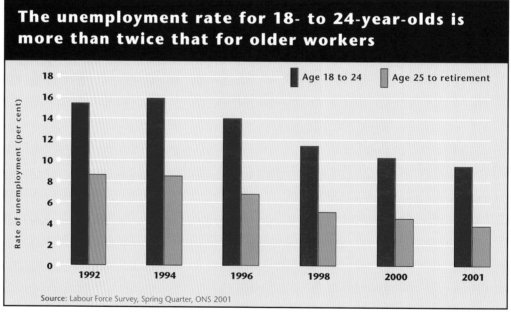

**The unemployment rate for 18- to 24-year-olds is
more than twice that for older workers**

Source: Labour Force Survey, Spring Quarter, ONS 2001

The first graph shows the number of unemployed people aged 16 to 24, as recorded each Spring, for each year between 1992 and 2000.

The second graph shows the rate of unemployment for those aged 18 to 24, compared with those aged 25 and over (up to retirement).

'Unemployment' is the ILO definition, which is now used for the official UK unemployment numbers and is obtained from the Labour Force Survey (LFS). It includes all those with no paid work in the survey week who were available to start work in the next fortnight and who either looked for work in the last month or were waiting to start a job already obtained. The ILO unemployment rate is the percentage of the economically active population who are unemployed on the ILO measure.

The data is not seasonally adjusted and refers to Great Britain.

Overall adequacy of the indicator: **medium**. *The LFS is a well-established, three-monthly government survey, designed to be representative of the population as a whole. This indicator does not, however, cover the 'economically inactive', which includes many of those on the lowest incomes, particularly young lone parents.*

On low rates of pay

Half a million young adults aged 18 to 21 continue to be paid less than half the male median hourly income

Below minimum wage   **Between half male median and minimum wage**

Employees aged 16 to 21 on hourly rates below half male median earnings (thousands)

	1998	1999	2000

Source: ONS statistics and NPI calculations

More than half of the young adults who earn less than half the male median hourly pay work in the distribution, hotel and catering trades

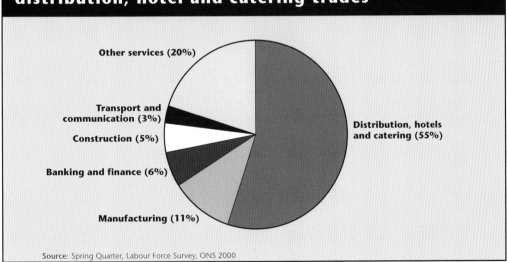

Other services (20%)

Transport and communication (3%)

Construction (5%)

Banking and finance (6%)

Manufacturing (11%)

Distribution, hotels and catering (55%)

Source: Spring Quarter, Labour Force Survey, ONS 2000

The first graph shows the estimated number of employees aged 18 to 21 who were paid below half the estimated male median hourly rate of pay in each year shown. It is divided between those earning less than the minimum wage and those earning above it but below half male median. In spring 2000, the half male median hourly rate was approximately £4.00 an hour. This figure was arrived at using published Labour Force Survey (LFS) statistics and interpolation. For the same year the minimum wage for 18- to 21-year-olds was £3.00 an hour.

Note that this graph has been changed from that published in previous reports due to data constraints imposed by the ONS. The data is derived from a combination of the LFS and the New Earnings Survey (NES), with adjustments by the ONS.

The second graph shows the distribution of employees aged 16 to 24 earning less than the half male median hourly pay, across different sectors of the economy.

Overall adequacy of the indicator: **limited.** *The LFS and NES are well-established government surveys, designed to be representative of the population as a whole. However, neither survey accurately measures low pay in its own right. The combined methodology attempts to adjust the figures to compensate.*

Not in education, training or work

Indicator
19

At 160,000 (9 per cent of the age group), the number of 16- to 18-year-olds not in education, training or work has remained broadly unchanged since 1993

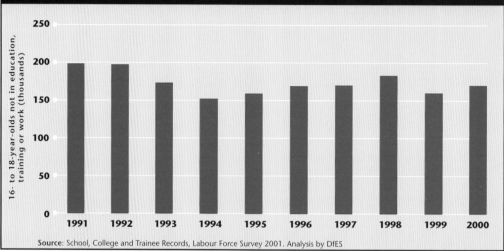

Source: School, College and Trainee Records, Labour Force Survey 2001. Analysis by DfES

A fifth of of 16- to 18-year-olds not in education, training or work have left home

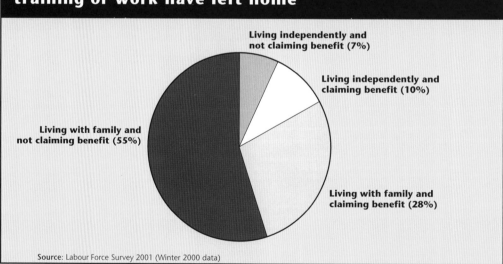

Source: Labour Force Survey 2001 (Winter 2000 data)

The first graph shows the number of 16- 18-year-olds not in education, training or employment. The data has been put together by DfES statisticians, combining the Labour Force Survey with school, college and trainee records.

Note that data for 2000 is provisional. Also, data for 1998 and 1999 was revised in 2001 in line with population changes.

The second graph is based on the Labour Force Survey alone. It takes all those found within the survey not to be in education, training or work and shows whether they are living independently (head of household, spouse, cohabitee or with other non-relative) or living with family (child, step-child, brother, sister, grandchild or other relation). The data also shows whether the young person is dependent on any of the following benefits: income support, jobseeker's allowance, sickness/disability benefit, housing or council tax benefit.

Note that comparisons cannot be made between figures for those not in education, training or work and unemployment statistics as it is possible to be both in education/training and unemployed at the same time.

Overall adequacy of the indicator: **high**. *The Labour Force Survey is a well-established, three-monthly government survey, designed to be representative of the population as a whole.*

Problem drug use

Indicator
20

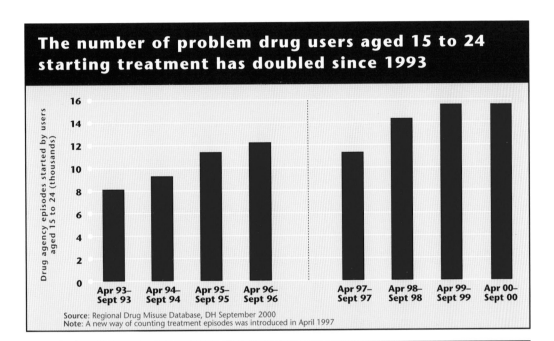

The number of problem drug users aged 15 to 24 starting treatment has doubled since 1993

Drug agency episodes started by users aged 15 to 24 (thousands)

| Apr 93– Sept 93 | Apr 94– Sept 94 | Apr 95– Sept 95 | Apr 96– Sept 96 | Apr 97– Sept 97 | Apr 98– Sept 98 | Apr 99– Sept 99 | Apr 00– Sept 00 |

Source: Regional Drug Misuse Database, DH September 2000
Note: A new way of counting treatment episodes was introduced in April 1997

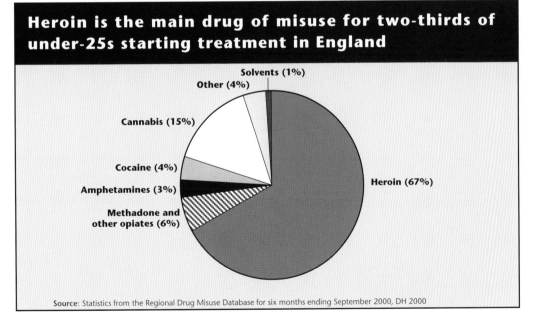

Heroin is the main drug of misuse for two-thirds of under-25s starting treatment in England

Solvents (1%)
Other (4%)
Cannabis (15%)
Cocaine (4%)
Amphetamines (3%)
Methadone and other opiates (6%)
Heroin (67%)

Source: Statistics from the Regional Drug Misuse Database for six months ending September 2000, DH 2000

The first graph shows the number of 15- to 24-year-olds in Great Britain starting an episode with any agency offering services to drug misusers. Note that a new way of counting treatment episodes was introduced in April 1997.

The data for Scotland for the latest year is based partly on actual returns and partly on estimates. This is due to 'missing data' in one of the databases.

The second graph shows the breakdown by drug type among users in England starting an agency episode for April to September 2000 (the most recent six months for which data is available). An 'episode' is defined as a person presenting to a treatment agency for the first time or after a break in contact of six months or more.

Overall adequacy of the indicator: **limited***. The numbers count individuals presenting for treatment in each six-month period, but do not include those in treatment who presented in an earlier six-month period. Furthermore, services such as needle exchange schemes, outreach work and most services for those in prison are excluded. Finally many problem drug users do not present for treatment at all.*

Suicide

Indicator 21

The number of suicides amongst young adults aged 15 to 24 has fallen in recent years in England and Wales, but not in Scotland

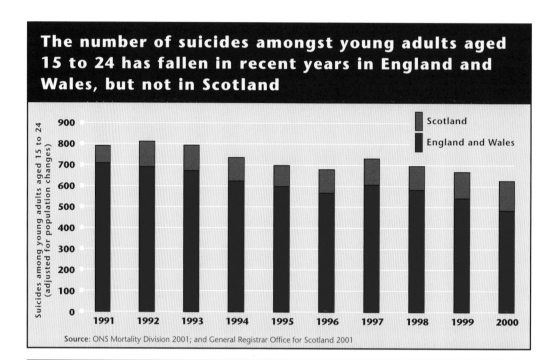

Source: ONS Mortality Division 2001; and General Registrar Office for Scotland 2001

Young men in the manual social classes are twice as likely to commit suicide as those in the non-manual classes

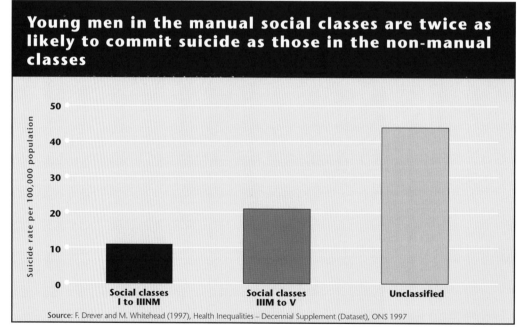

Source: F. Drever and M. Whitehead (1997), Health Inequalities – Decennial Supplement (Dataset), ONS 1997

The first graph shows the number of suicides in Great Britain, showing the statistics separately for England and Wales and for Scotland. Suicide data includes deaths recorded as 'undetermined', where there is an open verdict, and therefore includes deaths where suicide was the probable verdict as well as those where suicide was formally given as the verdict.

Note that the method used to record mortality in Scotland was revised in 2000. This may slightly affect data continuity.

The second graph relates to England and Wales only. It shows the suicide rate per 100,000 for men aged 20 to 24 for the years 1991–93, broken down by social class. The 'other' group includes both those for whom insufficient information was available to determine a social class and those 'without an occupation', including those with no previous job, students, full-time carers and/or dependent relatives, those permanently sick and mentally or physically disabled people.

*Overall adequacy of indicator: **medium**. However, classification of a death as suicide depends upon the practices of coroners' courts and is therefore potentially affected by administrative or procedural changes.*

Without a basic qualification

Indicator
22

The number of 19-year-olds without a basic qualification has remained similar throughout the second half of the 1990s, although this represents a decreasing proportion of the total population of 19-year-olds

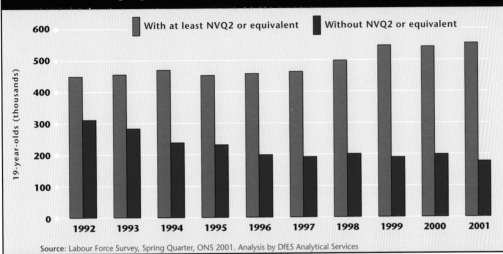

Source: Labour Force Survey, Spring Quarter, ONS 2001. Analysis by DfES Analytical Services

Nearly 10 per cent of 19-year-olds have no qualifications at all

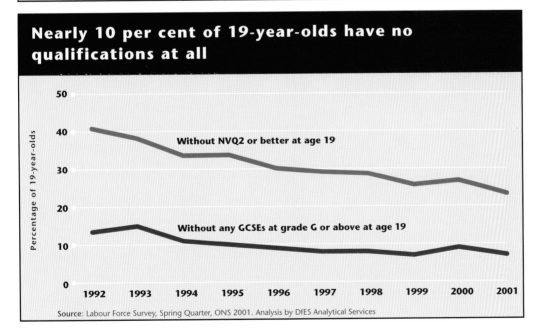

Source: Labour Force Survey, Spring Quarter, ONS 2001. Analysis by DfES Analytical Services

The first graph shows the number of 19-year-olds without a basic qualification. The second graph expresses this as a percentage of all 19-year-olds. It also shows the percentage of 19-year-olds with no qualification at all.

A basic qualification means an NVQ2 or equivalent (i.e. including five GCSEs at grade C or above; GNVQ level 2; two AS levels or one A level). 'Unqualified' means no GCSE passes at grade G or above and/or no NVQs. The data is for Great Britain. The data source is the Labour Force Survey (LFS).

*Overall assessment of the indicator: **high**. The LFS is a well-established, three-monthly survey designed to be representative of the population as whole. It should be noted, however, that there are breaks in the series in 1993 and 1996 due to changes in the questions asked within the LFS.*

With a criminal record

Indicator 23

The number of 18- to 20-year-olds found guilty of an indictable offence has remained broadly unchanged since 1993

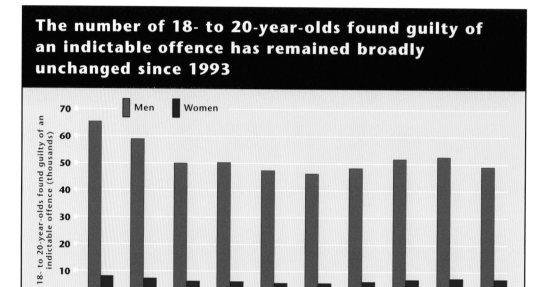

Source: Criminal Statistics , England and Wales, Home Office
Note: 2000 figures are provisional

Black young adults are seven times as likely as white young adults to be in prison

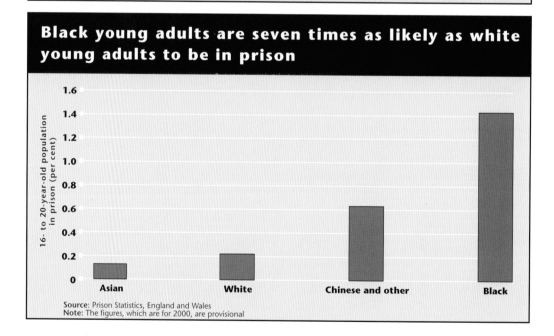

Source: Prison Statistics, England and Wales
Note: The figures, which are for 2000, are provisional

The first graph shows the number of young men and women aged 18 to 20 who were convicted of an indictable offence in each year. Figures for 2000 were provisional at the time of publication. The data relates to England and Wales.

The second graph shows the likelihood of being in prison under sentence across different ethnic groups in England and Wales in June 2000. In putting together prison data with population data, it has been assumed that the relative sizes of the ethnic groups in the 16- to 20-year-old prison population in England and Wales in 1998 can be mapped onto the total populations of different ethnic groups aged 15 to 20 in Great Britain in the 1991 census. 'Asians' include people from Bangladeshi, Indian and Pakistani communities. 'Chinese and other' includes people from other Asian communities, Chinese ethnic groups and other.

*Overall adequacy of the indicator: **medium**. The data is dependent upon administrative practices of the police and the judicial system. For example, according to Home Office Criminal Statistics (1995), rates of informal cautioning (which are not included in the graphs) have increased in recent years, which may have had a downward impact on the trends illustrated above.*

4 Adults

Why the indicators were chosen

Those aged from 25 to retirement age make up about half of the total population. Although they are in some ways the least vulnerable of all age groups, they are often under considerable and multiple pressures to support others, as well as themselves.

Exclusion from work

The first indicator is the 'number of people who would like paid work but do not have it'. This indicator recognises that it is not sufficient to look only at those officially unemployed since they are actually a minority of working age adults who would like to have a job.

The second indicator is the 'number of workless households in which no one has worked for two years or more'. As with individuals, certain sorts of households are particularly vulnerable to long-term worklessness. Lone parent households, households headed by someone sick or someone with a disability, and minority ethnic households all have an above average likelihood of long-term worklessness.[1] Long-term unemployment has many negative effects on health.[2]

Disadvantaged at work

The working conditions and the pay of some workers leave them only marginally better off than people without work, particularly if they are single and childless and therefore ineligible for in-work tax credits. The last twenty years has seen a gap open up between average earnings and the earnings of the lowest paid. The chosen low pay indicator is 'people earning less than half male median hourly pay'.

Frequent moves in and out of low paid employment has become the experience of many workers, predominantly those with below average skill levels. The chosen indicator of work insecurity is 'people making a new claim for unemployment benefit who were last claiming less than six months ago'. The indicator also looks at the number of workers in temporary employment.

The chosen indicator on training is the 'chance of receiving job-related training by level of qualifications', which examines the inequality in access to training between those with and without qualifications. Work-related training and gaining new qualifications are both means of reducing the chances of negative labour market outcomes.[3]

Health

The first health indicator is the 'number of local authorities where the death rate for under-65s is 10 per cent or more above the British average', providing an overall indicator of health inequalities.

The second indicator shows the 'proportion of working-age women who are obese'. Obesity is a major risk factor for a range of lethal diseases, from heart disease to cancers,[4] and, in the case of women, differs substantially by social class.

Depression is one of the most common forms of mental illness, and its effects can spread into all dimensions of a person's life, including their work, home and social environments. Triggers identified for development of depression include unemployment, redundancy or the threat of it, and financial difficulties.[5] The chosen indicator of mental health is '**adults classified as being at high risk of developing mental illness**', with the second graph showing how the incidence of depression varies by income.

What the indicators show

Falling unemployment but unchanged numbers of long-term workless households

The number of unemployed continues to fall and now stands at 1¹/2 million, around half the figure in 1993. In contrast, the numbers of 'economically inactive' people who want work has remained consistently above 2 million over the same period. The combined effect is that the total **number of people who would like to work** has fallen more slowly than the level of unemployed, from 5 million in 1993 to 3¹/2 million in 2001.

There has also been no fall in the number of **long-term workless households**, which currently stands at 2 million compared to 1¹/2 million in 1993.

Within these overall totals, significant differences remain between groups. People of Caribbean, Pakistani, Bangladeshi and African ethnic backgrounds are twice as likely to be excluded from work as the white population. Almost half of lone parents did not have paid work in 2001 compared to one in twenty couples with children.

Some of the groups most excluded from work – the long-term unemployed, lone parents, people with disabilities and the over 50s – are the target of New Deal policies to increase their labour market participation. It is noteworthy that the published targets for these programmes are mostly short term (to 2002) and thus inevitably relatively small – totalling around a third of a million – compared to the 3¹/2 million people in the labour market as a whole who would like to work.[6] The only long-term target is for lone parents, where the 2010 target of 70 per cent employment compares with the current level of 55 per cent.

Low pay still appears to be a major problem

Since the introduction of the national minimum wage in April 1999, there appears to have been a sharp fall in the numbers being paid below this level. In 2000, an estimated ¹/4 million employees aged 22 and over were being paid below £3.60 per hour.[7] This compares with an estimated 1¹/2 million in 1998.

However, a rather different picture emerges using thresholds which are above the level of the minimum wage but still a low rate of pay. For example, an estimated 1¹/2 million employees aged 22 and over were being paid less than half male median earnings (around £4 per hour) in 2000, down from around 2 million in 1998.

What therefore appears to be happening to people on low rates of pay is that those previously paid below the level of the minimum wage have had their pay increased to the minimum wage or just above, whilst those on low pay but above the level of the minimum wage have been largely unaffected. It follows that the precise level at which the minimum wage is set in the future is crucial.

In this context, it is worth noting the current difficulties in obtaining data about low pay: independent analysis of the Labour Force Survey low pay data is no longer possible because the Office of National Statistics has declared it unreliable[8] and, because of their need to adjust the data, details utilising the Spring 2001 survey were not available at the time of going to press.[9] Furthermore, their published statistics only cover the period 1998 to 2000, with no data being available for earlier years.

Levels of insecure employment seem to have stabilised

Around four in ten people who make a new claim for jobseeker's allowance last claimed less than six months ago. These figures have been stable since 1997, but are still well above the levels in 1990. The number of employees in temporary contracts shows a similar pattern. So, **insecurity of employment** remains a bigger problem than in the past.

Those without qualifications are still three times less likely to receive **work-related training** than those with qualifications, and the fewer qualifications a person has, the less likely they are to receive such training.

Continuing health inequalities

Having been rising for much of the last decade, the geographic concentration of health inequalities – measured according to the number of local authority areas with mortality rates which are significantly above average – fell in 2000. Although encouraging, it remains to be seen whether this is part of a sustained pattern. Within Great Britain, Scotland has by far the highest proportion of **premature deaths** for men: a third of its local authorities had high male mortality rates, compared with one in ten for Great Britain as a whole.

Our other health indicators – **obesity, longstanding illness/disability and risk of mental illness** – have not changed significantly over the last ten years. But they continue to illustrate significant inequalities. Unskilled manual workers are $1^1/2$ times as likely to have a long-standing illness or disability as members of the professional classes. The poorest two-fifths of the population are $1^1/2$ times as likely to be at risk of a mental illness than the richest two-fifths. And women from social classes IIIM to V are somewhat more likely to be obese than women from social classes I to IIINM (although there is no such pattern for men).

In terms of specific initiatives, the Government has chosen to focus on the geographical dimension of health inequalities by establishing 26 Health Action Zones which are intended to cover 13 million people. Clearly, not all disadvantaged people live in disadvantaged areas, and one issue for future monitoring will therefore be the extent to which the Government's primarily geographic approach reduces the overall inequalities or whether new non-geographic initiatives are also needed.

Selected major initiatives under way

Indicators	Policy	Start date	Key department	Key delivery agency	Budget/target/comments
24 Individuals wanting paid work *and* **25 Households without work for two years or more**	New Deal for the Long-Term Unemployed	June 1998: introduced for those 25 and over. April 2001: extended to the under 25s.	DfES/DWP	Employment Service	Aims to move 38,000 people unemployed for two years or more into work in 1999/00, 32,000 in 2000/01, and 62,000 in 2001/02. Government figures are that 63,000 people found jobs between June 1998 and December 2000. Budgets of £24m in 1998/99, £108m in 1999/00, £128m in 2000/01, £208m in 2001/02, £248m in 2003/04.
	New Deal for Disabled People	September 1998: introduced. April 2001: extended.	DfES/DWP	Employment Service	Aims to move 85,000 disabled people into work in 1999/00, 1,000 in 2000/01 and 5,000 in 2001/02 (these include places of other disabled people on inactive benefits). Budgets of £5m in 1998/99 and £20m each year from 2000 to 2004.
	New Deal for Lone Parents	July 1997: prototype. October 1998: national rollout. April 2001: extended. October 2001: extended.	DfES/DWP	Employment Service	Aims to achieve an overall 70% employment for lone parents by 2010, including 15,000 into work in 1999/2000, 29,000 in 2000/01 and 62,000 in 2001/02. Government figures state that 150,000 lone parents have received help, with 75,000 finding jobs (as of December 2000). In 1998, the programme focused on those lone parents making a new or repeat claim for income support. In 2001, the initiative was extended in a number of ways, for example providing financial support for training and childcare, as well as to all lone parents claiming benefits or on low income. Budgets of £20m in 1998/99, £40m in 1999/00, £50m in 2000/01, £100m in 2001/02, £180m in 2002/03 and £250m in 2003/04.
	New Deal for the Over-50s	November 1999: pathfinders. April 2000: implementation.	DfES/DWP	Employment Service	Aims to move 14,000 over-50s into work in 2000/01 and 30,000 in 2001/02. Government figures are that 24,000 had gone back to work as of December 2000. It is a voluntary scheme and, overall, 1 million people are eligible to participate. Includes payments of a tax-free employment credit, a training grant, and support and advice. Budgets of £5m for 1999/00 and £20m for each year until 2004.
	New Deal for Partners of Unemployed People	February 1999: started. April 2000: becomes mandatory.	DfES/DWP	Employment Service	Aims to move 3,000 eligible people into work in 2000/01 and 3,000 in 2001/02. Budgets of £5m for 1999/00 and £20m for each subsequent year until 2004.
26 On low rates of pay	National minimum wage	April 1999: introduced. October 2000: uprated. October 2001: uprated. October 2002: to be uprated.	DTI	Inland Revenue and employers	When introduced, set at £3.60 per hour for those over 22 years, unless in an exempt category or on a registered training scheme (in which case only £3.20). Increases to £3.70 in October 2000, £4.10 in October 2001 and £4.20 in October 2002. The Low Pay Commission estimates that the original national minimum wage affected 1.3 million jobs, potentially rising to 1.5 million after the October 2001 increases.
	Working families tax credit	October 1999: introduced. October 2000: uprated. April 2001: uprated. October 2001: to be uprated.	Treasury and DWP	Inland Revenue and employers	Aims to benefit 1.5 million families (twice as many as family credit). When first introduced, guaranteed a weekly gross income of £200 for a family with one full time worker. No tax until £235 per week for families with one full-timer (55p taper, down from 70p under Family Credit). The level of the credit depends on the number of children, how many hours worked (the minimum is 16 hours), childcare costs and levels of savings. Increases to £208 in October 2000, £214 in April 2001, £225 in October 2001 and £225 in October 2001. As from April 2001 no tax is paid until earnings of £250 are reached, for a family with one full timer. As of February 2001, 1¼ million families were claiming. The 2001 budget estimated that families on WFTC were on average £30 a week better off than they were under family credit. Provides £5bn of help each year to 1.4 million working families from 2000/01. This represents an extra £1.4bn compared to family credit.
29 Premature death **30 Obesity** **31 Long-standing illness or disability**	Health Action Zones	April 1998: first wave. April 1999: second wave.	DH	Health partnerships (NHS, Local authorities, voluntary and private sectors)	Aims to improve health and to modernise services in areas of high health need and deprivation. There are 26 zones that will operate for 7 years and collectively cover around 13 million people. A budget of £320m for the three years from 1999/00.
32 Depression	Modernising Mental Health Services	1999	DH	Health authorities	Aims to reduce mental health problems, including depression. The only specific target is on suicides: to reduce the rate of suicides by at least 20% by 2010. A budget of £700m for 1999 to 2002

Individuals wanting paid work

Indicator
24

The overall number of people who would like paid work continues to fall. But, whereas the numbers officially unemployed have halved since 1993, the numbers who are 'economically inactive but would like work' have remained unchanged

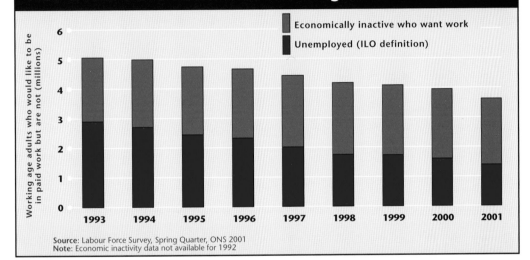

Source: Labour Force Survey, Spring Quarter, ONS 2001
Note: Economic inactivity data not available for 1992

People of Caribbean, Pakistani, Bangladeshi and African ethnicity are much more likely than the rest of the population to be out of work but wanting work

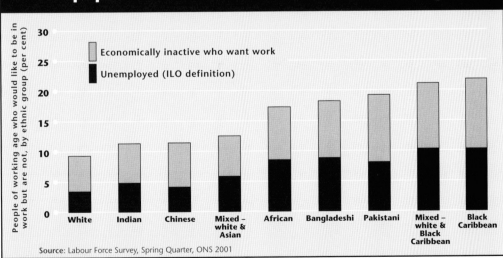

Source: Labour Force Survey, Spring Quarter, ONS 2001

The first graph shows the number of working age people wanting work. It is divided between the unemployed (as defined by the ILO) and those counted as 'economically inactive' who nevertheless want work. This latter group includes people not available to start work for some time and those not actively seeking work. The data is based on a question in the Labour Force Survey (LFS) asking the economically inactive whether they would like paid work or not. The data relates to the United Kingdom.

The second graph shows the same data for Great Britain by different ethnic groups in Spring 2001. The data relates to Great Britain. It looks at the whole labour force from 16 to retirement age and so includes 'young adults' as well.

*Overall adequacy of the indicator: **high**. The LFS is a well-established, three-monthly government survey of 60,000 households, designed to be representative of the population as a whole.*

Households without work
for two years or more

Indicator
25

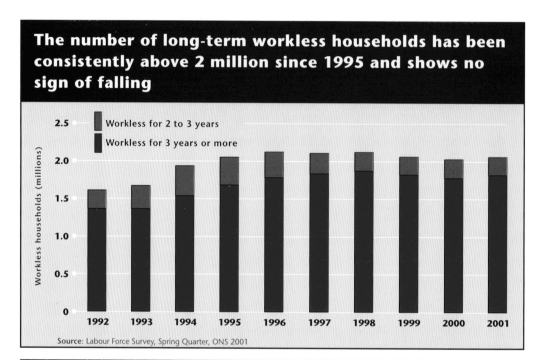

The number of long-term workless households has been consistently above 2 million since 1995 and shows no sign of falling

Source: Labour Force Survey, Spring Quarter, ONS 2001

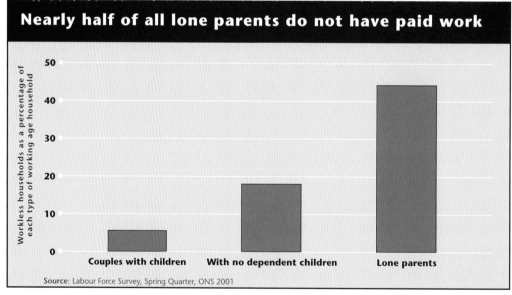

Nearly half of all lone parents do not have paid work

Source: Labour Force Survey, Spring Quarter, ONS 2001

The first graph shows the total number of households where no-one has worked for two years or more. The upper part of the bar shows how many have been workless for between two and three years. The lower part shows how many have been workless for three years or more. The second graph shows the number of individuals in workless households analysed by family type.

Data is for the Spring quarter of each year and relates to the United Kingdom. It looks at the whole labour force from age 16 upwards and so applies to 'young adults' as well.

*Overall adequacy of the indicator: **high**. The Labour Force Survey is a well-established, three-monthly government survey of 60,000 households designed to be representative of the population as a whole.*

On low rates of pay

**Indicator
26**

The number of people paid below half male median hourly pay has fallen, but by much less than the numbers paid below the national minimum wage

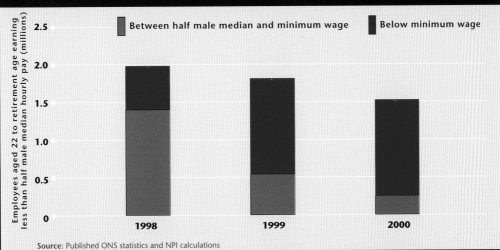

Source: Published ONS statistics and NPI calculations

There are a higher proportion of low paid workers in the distribution, hotels and catering sector than in any other sector

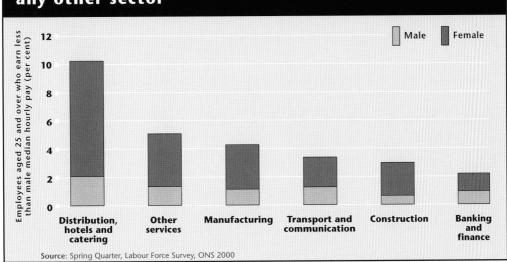

Source: Spring Quarter, Labour Force Survey, ONS 2000

The first graph shows the estimated number of employees aged 22 to retirement age who were paid below half the estimated male median hourly rate of pay in each year shown. It is divided between those earning less than the minimum wage and those earning above it but below half male median. In spring 2000, the half male median hourly rate was approximately £4.00 an hour. This figure was arrived at using published Labour Force Survey(LFS) statistics and interpolation. For the same year the minimum wage for those aged 22 was £3.60 an hour.

Note that this graph has been changed from that published in previous reports due to data constraints imposed by the ONS. The data is derived from a combination of the LFS and the New Earnings Survey (NES) with adjustments by the ONS.

The second graph shows the proportion of workers aged 25 and over who were paid below half male median income by industry sector.

Overall adequacy of the indicator: **limited**. *The LFS and NES are well-established government surveys, designed to be representative of the population as a whole. However, neither survey accurately measures low pay in its own right. The combined methodology attempts to adjust the figures to compensate.*

Insecure at work

Indicator
27

Four out of every 10 people making a new claim for jobseeker's allowance (JSA) were last claiming less than six months ago. This proportion has not changed much in recent years

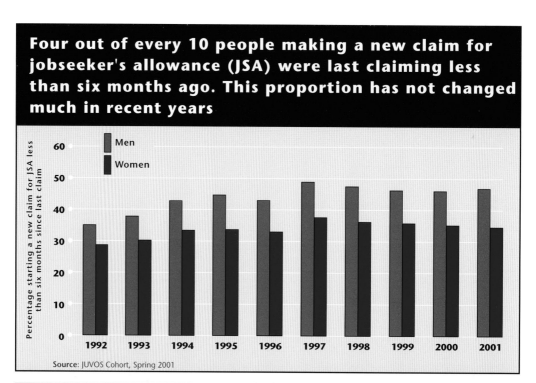

Source: JUVOS Cohort, Spring 2001

The number of people on temporary contracts has levelled off since its peak in 1997

Source: Labour Force Survey, Spring Quarter, ONS 2001

The first graph shows the probability that someone who makes a new claim for jobseeker's allowance was last claiming that benefit less than six months previously. Figures are shown separately for men and women. The data relates to Great Britain and is taken from the Spring quarters of the Joint Unemployment and Vacancies Operating System (JUVOS) cohort.

The second graph shows how the number of temporary workers who are of working age has changed since 1992. A temporary employee is one who said that his/her main job is non-permanent in one of the following ways: fixed period contracts; agency temping; casual work; seasonal work; and other temporary work. The data is based on non-seasonally adjusted Spring quarters of the Labour Force Survey. The data relates to the United Kingdom.

*Overall adequacy of the indicator: **medium**. While the claimant count data is sound, the narrower definition of unemployment that it represents means that it understates the extent of short-term working interspersed with spells of joblessness.*

Without access
to training

Indicator
28

Less than one in ten people without qualifications receive any job related training

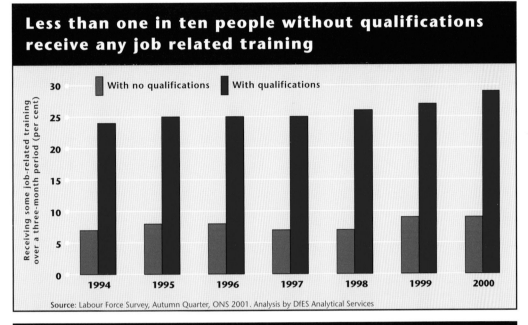

Source: Labour Force Survey, Autumn Quarter, ONS 2001. Analysis by DfES Analytical Services

The fewer qualifications a person has, the less likely they are to receive training at work

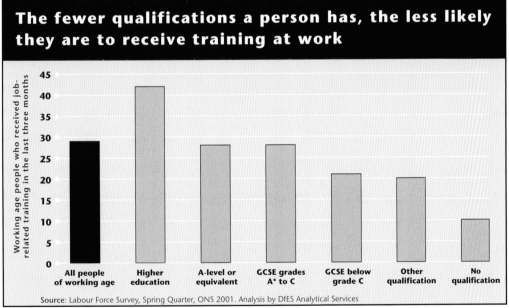

Source: Labour Force Survey, Spring Quarter, ONS 2001. Analysis by DfES Analytical Services

The first graph shows the proportion of employees aged 25 to retirement age who have received some job-related training in the previous three months according to whether they have some qualification or not. The qualifications include both current qualifications (e.g. GCSEs) and qualifications which have been awarded in the past (e.g. O levels). The data refers to Great Britain.

The second graph shows the proportion of employees of working age who have received training in the last three months by the level of their highest qualification. The data is for 2001 and refers to the United Kindgom.

In both cases, the training includes that paid for by employers and by employees themselves.

*Overall adequacy of the indicator: **medium**. The Labour Force Survey is a well-established, three-monthly government survey, designed to be representative of the population as a whole. But a single, undifferentiated notion of 'training,' without reference to its length or nature, lessens the value of the indicator.*

Premature death

Indicator
29

After rising throughout most of the decade, geographic concentrations of premature deaths amongst men under age 65 may now to be falling

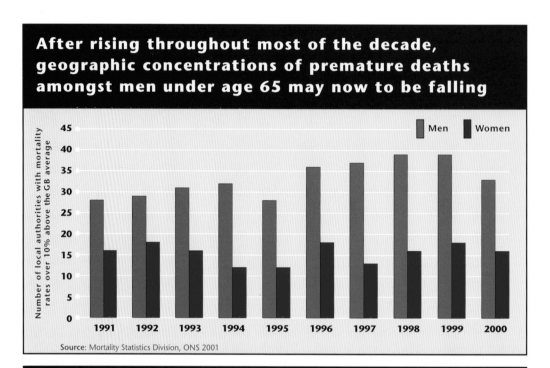

Men ■ Women ■

Number of local authorities with mortality rates over 10% above the GB average

1991 1992 1993 1994 1995 1996 1997 1998 1999 2000

Source: Mortality Statistics Division, ONS 2001

Scotland has the highest proportion of local authorities with high male mortality rates

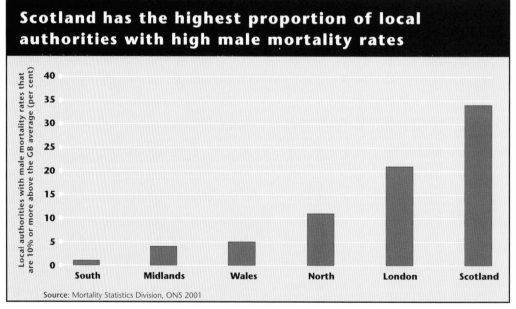

Local authorities with male mortality rates that are 10% or more above the GB average (per cent)

South   Midlands   Wales   North   London   Scotland

Source: Mortality Statistics Division, ONS 2001

The first graph shows, separately for men and women, the number of local authorities where the age standardised mortality rate (based on the European Standard Population) for those aged under 65 is at least 10 per cent above the Great Britain rate for the year in question. The strict definition of '10 per cent above average' is that the lower bound of the 95 per cent interval estimate for the authority, and the upper bound of the 95 per cent interval estimate for Great Britain as whole, differ by 10 per cent of the British average.

The second graph shows where those 33 local authorities which had mortality rates amongst men aged under 65 which were more than 10 per cent above national average are located.

Note that, over the period 1991 to 2000, premature deaths fell by some 16 per cent for men on average and by 12 per cent for women.

*Overall adequacy of the indicator: **high**. The underlying data are deaths organised according to the local authority area of residence of the deceased by the ONS in England and Wales and by the Registrar General for Scotland.*

Obesity

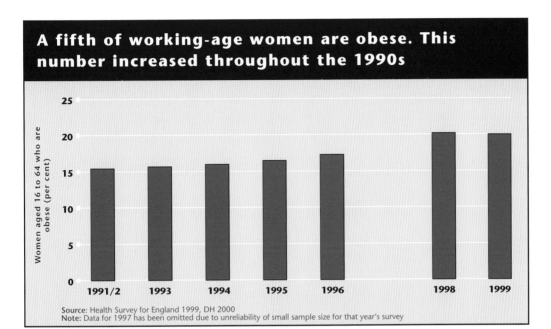

A fifth of working-age women are obese. This number increased throughout the 1990s

Women aged 16 to 64 who are obese (per cent)

1991/2 1993 1994 1995 1996 1998 1999

Source: Health Survey for England 1999, DH 2000
Note: Data for 1997 has been omitted due to unreliability of small sample size for that year's survey

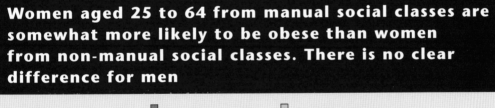

Women aged 25 to 64 from manual social classes are somewhat more likely to be obese than women from non-manual social classes. There is no clear difference for men

Social classes I–IIINM   Social classes IIIM–V

Men and women aged 25 to 64 who are obese (per cent)

Men   Women

Source: Health Survey for England 1999, DH 2000

The first graph shows the number of women aged 16 to 64 who are obese, where obesity is defined as those with a body mass index greater than 30 kg/m^2.

The second graph shows the variation in 1999 across social classes in the percentage of men and women aged 25 to 64 who were obese.

The data relates to England only.

Overall adequacy of the indicator: **high**. *The Health Survey for England is a large survey which is designed to be representative of the population in England as a whole.*

Limiting long-standing illness or disability

Nearly 4 million adults aged 45 to 64 suffer a long-standing illness or disability which limits their activity. The numbers of men and women are similar

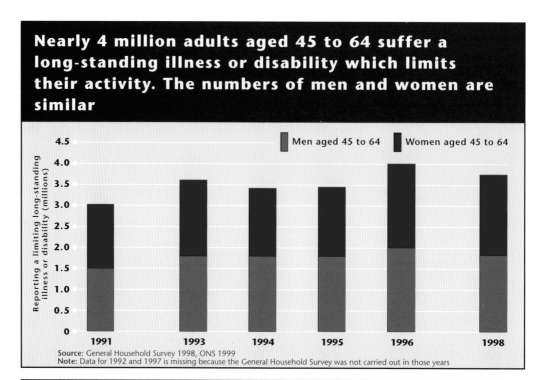

Source: General Household Survey 1998, ONS 1999
Note: Data for 1992 and 1997 is missing because the General Household Survey was not carried out in those years

Adults in junior and manual occupational groups are more at risk of a limiting long-standing illness or disability than those in professional, managerial and other non-manual work

Source: General Household Survey 1998, ONS 1999

The first graph shows the number of adults aged 45 to 64 who report having a long-term illness or disability that limits the activities they are able to carry out. The question asked is "Do you have any long-standing illness, disability or infirmity? Longstanding is anything that has troubled you over a period of time or that is likely to affect you over a period of time. Does this illness or disability limit your activities in any way?"

The second graph shows how levels of self-reported ill health and disability varies between occupational groups.

The data relates to Great Britain.

*Overall adequacy of the indicator: **medium**. While the General Household Survey is a well-established government survey designed to be representative of the population as a whole, the inevitable variation in what respondents understand and interpret as 'long-standing' and 'limiting activity', diminishes the value of the indicator.*

Mental health

Indicator
32

The proportion of adults aged 16 to 64 who are at high risk of developing a mental illness remained broadly stable throughout the 1990s. Women are more at risk than men

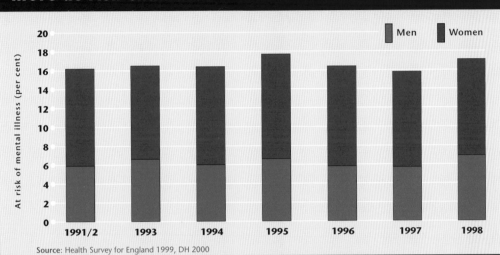

Source: Health Survey for England 1999, DH 2000

People with lower incomes are more likely to be at risk of developing a mental illness than those on average and higher incomes

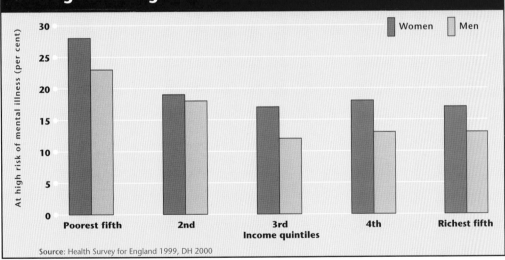

Source: Health Survey for England 1999, DH 2000

The first graph shows the proportion of adults aged 16 to 64 who are classified as being at high risk of developing a mental illness. This is determined by asking informants a number of questions about general levels of happiness, depression, anxiety and sleep disturbance over the previous four weeks, which are designed to detect possible psychiatric morbidity. A score is constructed from the responses, and the figures published show those with a score of 4 or more. This is referred to as a 'high GHQ12 score'.

The second graph shows the variation of the above in 1999 across income groups.

The data relates to England only.

Overall adequacy of the indicator: **high**. *The Health Survey for England is a large survey which is designed to be representative of the population in England as a whole.*

5 Older people

Why the indicators were chosen
Economic circumstances
Although pensioners on average enjoy better incomes than they have in the past, this rising average conceals a large minority who have no additional resources other than the state retirement pension and means tested benefits. The first indicator of pensioners' economic circumstances is the '**number of pensioners without a private income**' (i.e. no income other than the state retirement pension and state benefits).[1]

The second chosen indicator for pensioner economic circumstances is the '**level of expenditure on essentials**', tracked separately for pensioners solely relying on income from the state and for other pensioners with greater incomes.

Health and well-being
As with other age groups, health problems amongst older people are not evenly distributed but are concentrated amongst the poorest. While life expectancy has been increasing overall, in many cases the number of years free of sickness and pain have not.[2]

Failing health is an inevitable consequence of growing older, but some of the effects of poor health can be avoided, and preventative health care can reduce the overall burden of ill health suffered. Older people occupy much of the substandard housing in Britain, and the link between ill health and housing is strong for this group. This is particularly important because many older people spend such a lot of time at home. The first health-related indicator is the '**number of excess winter deaths**' amongst older people, which also includes a graph showing the relationship between poor insulation and low income amongst older people.

Many disabled people are aged over 60.[3] The second indicator is the '**proportion of older people reporting ill health or a disability which limits their activities**', with the second graph showing the disparity across occupational groups.

Many older people suffer anxiety and depression, caused and compounded by bereavement, and indeed retirement itself, which for many is a disorientating and stressful experience. One symptom of anxiety and depression is fear of leaving the house and the third indicator is the '**proportion of older people feeling unsafe out alone after dark**'.

Access to services
The quality and appropriateness of services that older people receive is critical to their well-being and quality of life.

Both the quality of the experience older people have at home and the feasibility of their remaining at home will depend on the support that they receive.[4] The first indicator is the '**proportion of those aged 75 and over who receive help from social services to live at home**'.

The second indicator of access to services is '**pensioner households without a telephone**'. Telephone access for older people varies with income and is an important means of connection to the outside world, particularly to family and friends, as well as providing access to a range of services. Most of the population believe that a telephone is now a necessity of modern life.[5]

What the indicators show
Little change in pensioner poverty as of 1999/2000
The number of pensioners with no income other than their state pension and state benefits continues to remain within the 1.2 to 1.4 million range. This represents 20 per cent of all single pensioners and 10 per cent of all pensioner couples. Although numbers fell somewhat in

1999/00, this is not considered significant and a sustained fall is not thought to be likely until and unless the Government's policies aimed at encouraging greater use of private pensions start having an effect in the longer term.

In 1999/00, around 20 per cent of the pensioner population were in the bottom fifth of the income distribution (after housing costs), unchanged from the previous year. This lack of change is not surprising – although the Government introduced the minimum income guarantee (MIG) for pensioners in April 1999, the levels at which it did so were such that pensioners solely reliant on the state would still remain in the bottom fifth of the income distribution.[6]

The proportion of pensioners on low incomes differed according to both age and marital status. Whereas there are large numbers of older pensioners and younger single pensioners on low incomes, there are significantly fewer younger pensioner couples. Indeed, only 15 per cent of pensioner couples aged 75 and under were in the poorest fifth of the population, which is actually less than the proportion of working age adults and children.

In April 2001, the Government substantially increased the levels of the minimum income guarantee.[7] These amounts could be sufficient to lift many pensioners and particularly single pensioners out of the bottom fifth of the income distribution. This would depend on high rates of take-up and such figures are currently only analysed 18 months in arrears.[8] It would, of course, also depend on what happens to the incomes of the rest of the population.

Finally, spending on essentials by pensioner households who mainly depend on the state pension increased by 15 per cent in real terms between 1995/96 and 1999/00, compared with an increase of 10 per cent by better off pensioners.

A mixed picture in terms of access to services

The proportion of elderly people aged 75 and over who receive **support from social services** to help them live at home continues to fall, and is now two-thirds of what it was at the peak in 1994. Furthermore, county councils and unitary authorities appear to support far fewer households than either urban or Welsh authorities. This is despite the government's 'Better Services for Vulnerable People' initiative.

In contrast, the proportion of pensioner households **without a telephone** continues to fall, and is now a quarter of the levels of a decade ago. This does, however, still represent 200,000 households and pensioners who are mainly dependent on state pensions are still three times more likely to be without a telephone than other pensioner groups.

Poorer pensioners are also around twice as likely to live in badly insulated housing as the best-off pensioners. Although there is no direct causal link between the lack of insulation and **excess winter deaths**, between 20,000 to 50,000 more pensioners die in winter months each year than on average in other months and the figures were substantially higher in the second half of the 1990s than in the first half.

It is noteworthy that all of the statistics above have changed substantially over the last decade, with some getting better (for example, lack of telephones) and others getting worse (for example, support from social services). This suggests that changes in society are having an impact on the quality of life of older people. We conclude that the problem of exclusion from essential services – both public and private – is a subject with which the Government could usefully concern itself over the next few years. This could be part of a wider debate about what (apart from the core subject of income levels) poverty and social exclusion actually means for older people.

Selected major initiatives under way

Indicators	Policy	Start date	Key department	Key delivery agency	Budget/target/comments
33 No private income	Minimum income guarantee	April 1999: introduced. April 2000: uprated. April 2001: uprated.	DWP/Treasury	Benefits Agency	From April 1999: £75 a week for single pensioners and £116.60 for pensioner couples, representing increases of around £4 and £7 respectively over the levels of Income Support that were previously available. From April 2000: increased to £78.45 for single pensioners and £121.95 a week for pensioner couples. From April 2001: increased to £92.15 and £140.55 respectively. Under the Pensioners credit scheme (2003), the amounts will rise to £100 and £154 respectively. Available to anyone with an income below the threshold and with savings of no more than £12,000 (April 2001). The government estimates that 2 million pensioners are eligible. A take-up campaign was undertaken during 2000. 2.4m people were contacted and 110,000 claims were made. Annual budget of around £4bn (2000/01).
	Winter Fuel Payments (part of Fuel Poverty Initiative)	1997/98: introduced. 2000/01: uprated.	DWP/Treasury	Benefits Agency	Eligible households received £100 in 1999/00 and £200 in 2000/01 and in the following year. All pensioners in receipt of the State Retirement Pension or a social security benefit (excluding Child, Housing and Council Tax Benefits) are eligible. Total government spending was £1.76b for 2000/01
38 Help from social services	Better Services for Vulnerable People Initiative	October 1997. April 1999: joint investment plans for older people.	DH	Health authorities and local authorities jointly	£650m over 3 years for the prevention and rehabilitation services. Requires all local and health authorities to draw up Joint Investment Plans (JIPs) to co-ordinate development of services with the aims of ensuring necessary provision while minimising unnecessary admissions to hospitals and care centres.

No private income

Over 1 million pensioners (20 per cent of single pensioners and 8 per cent of pensioner couples in 1999/00) rely on the state retirement pension and state benefits alone

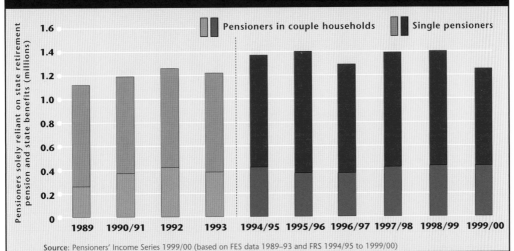

Source: Pensioners' Income Series 1999/00 (based on FES data 1989–93 and FRS 1994/95 to 1999/00)

Pensioner couples aged 75 and under are less heavily concentrated in the bottom half of the income distribution than other pensioners

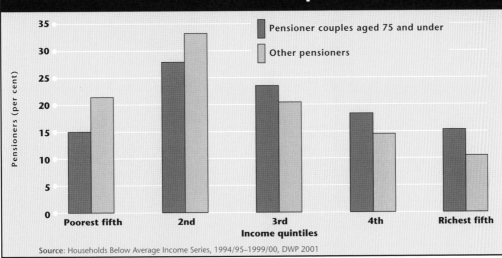

Source: Households Below Average Income Series, 1994/95–1999/00, DWP 2001

The first graph shows the number of pensioner families (individuals in pensioner benefit units) with no income other than the state retirement pension and state benefits. The data comes from the Pensioners' Incomes Series and is based partly on the Family Expenditure Survey (FES) (which relates to the UK), and partly on the Family Resources Survey (which relates to Great Britain). Note that direct comparisons should not be made between FES and FRS based results due to differences in coverage, definitions and survey instruments.

The second graph shows the distribution of pensioners across the income quintiles, split by pensioner type and age. The data comes from the Family Resources Survey (FRS) and relates to Great Britain.

Overall adequacy of the indicator: **high.** *The FES and FRS are both well-established government surveys, designed to be representative of the population as a whole. However, since they only cover people living in private households, and not residential institutions (such as nursing homes), they do leave out a significant group of older people.*

Spending on 'essentials'

Indicator
34

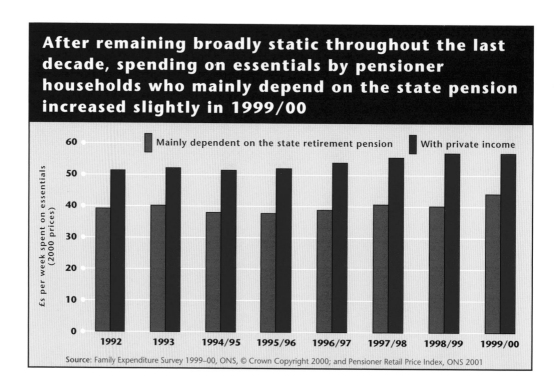

After remaining broadly static throughout the last decade, spending on essentials by pensioner households who mainly depend on the state pension increased slightly in 1999/00

Source: Family Expenditure Survey 1999–00, ONS, © Crown Copyright 2000; and Pensioner Retail Price Index, ONS 2001

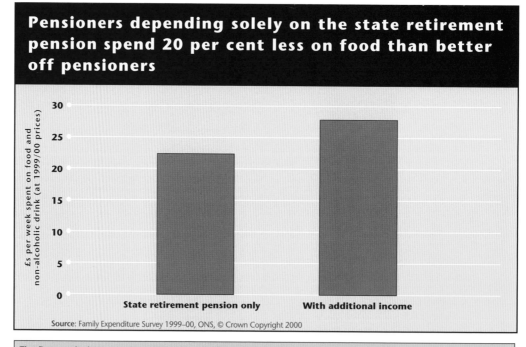

Pensioners depending solely on the state retirement pension spend 20 per cent less on food than better off pensioners

Source: Family Expenditure Survey 1999–00, ONS, © Crown Copyright 2000

The first graph shows pensioners' weekly spending on 'essential' items of expenditure (besides housing) for pensioners mainly dependent on the state retirement pension and for pensioners with other sources of income. The categories of expenditure counted as 'essential' include food, fuel, clothing and footwear, and household goods. Note that some spending on other categories such as travel may also be essential though they have not been included.

The figures are per person. In the case of pensioner couple households, this has meant dividing their expenditure in two and assuming that spending is equally divided across the household. The series are at 2000 prices and have been deflated using pensioner retail price indices separately for one-person and two-person pensioner households.

The second graph shows spending per head on food in pensioner households split by those whose income comes from the state retirement pension only and those who have other sources on income on top. Data is at 1999/00 prices. The data is unweighted.

*Overall adequacy of the indicator: **medium**. The Family Expenditure Survey is a well-established government survey, designed to be representative of the population as a whole. However, the spending categories chosen do not necessarily cover all essential spending, and include some items which might be considered non-essential. The data shown is therefore a proxy for spending on essentials by pensioner households.*

Excess winter deaths

Indicator
35

Each year, depending on the harshness of winter, 20,000 to 45,000 more people aged 65 or over die in winter months than in other months

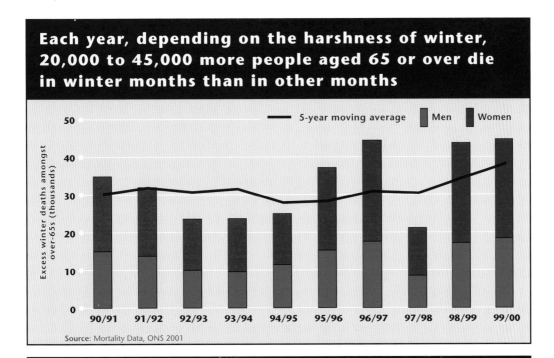

Source: Mortality Data, ONS 2001

The poorest pensioners are almost twice as likely to be in energy inefficient housing as the best off pensioners

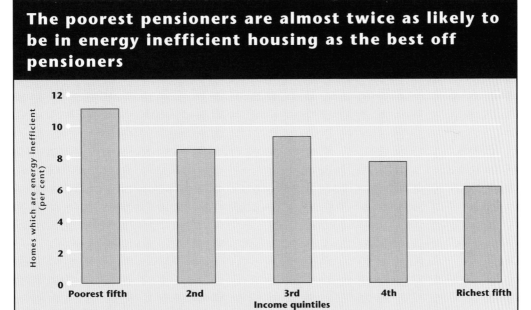

Source: English House Conditions Survey, DETR 1999

The first graph shows excess winter deaths each year in the 65 and above age group, where 'excess winter deaths' is defined as the difference between the number of deaths which occurred in winter (December to March) and the average number of deaths during the preceeding four months (August to November) and the subsequent four months (April to July). The graph also shows a five-year moving average, which is less affected by year-by-year fluctuations due to particularly cold and warm winters. The data is for England and Wales.

The second graph shows the percentage of pensioner households in each quintile (fifth) of the pensioner income distribution that live in an energy inefficient home. The energy efficiency of a household is measured by looking at the cost of heating per unit of floor space. The energy ratings given to households are a measure of the annual unit cost of heating the dwelling to a standard regime.

*Overall adequacy of the indicator: **medium**. Whilst the data sources used here are reliable ones, there is no data providing evidence of a direct causal relationship between winter deaths and energy inefficient housing.*

Limiting long-standing illness or disability

Indicator
36

Around 4 million adults aged 65 and over (a quarter of the age group) report a long-standing illness or disability

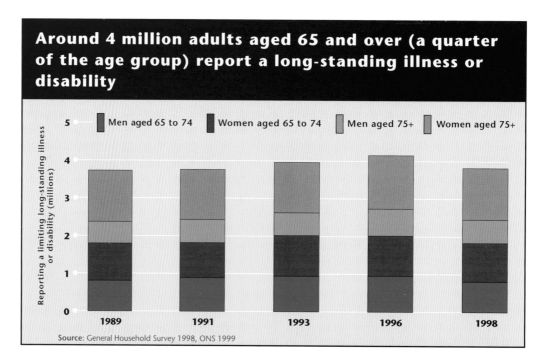

Source: General Household Survey 1998, ONS 1999

Men aged 65 and over who worked in manual trades are somewhat more likely to suffer a long-standing illness or disability than those with non-manual work histories. There is no such pattern for women

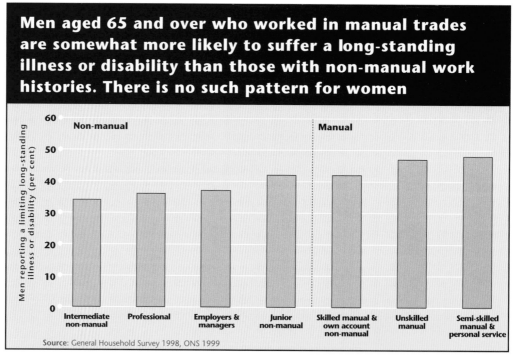

Source: General Household Survey 1998, ONS 1999

The first graph shows the number of older people aged 65 and over who report having a long-term illness or a disability that limits the activities they are able to carry out. The question asked was "Do you have any long-standing illness, disability or infirmity? Long-standing is anything that has troubled you over a period of time or that is likely to affect you over a period of time. Does this illness or disability limit your activities in any way?"

The second graph shows how levels of self-reported ill health and disability vary between occupational groups amongst men aged 65 and over. The data relates to Great Britain.

*Overall adequacy of the indicator: **medium**. While the General Household Survey is a well-established government survey designed to be representative of the population as a whole, the inevitable variation in what respondents understand and interpret as 'long-standing' and 'limiting activity', diminishes the value of the indicator. Furthermore, for women, the social-class classifications are not particularly sensitive to their real socio-economic circumstances.*

Anxiety

Indicator
37

Women aged 60 or over are twice as likely to feel unsafe out at night than men

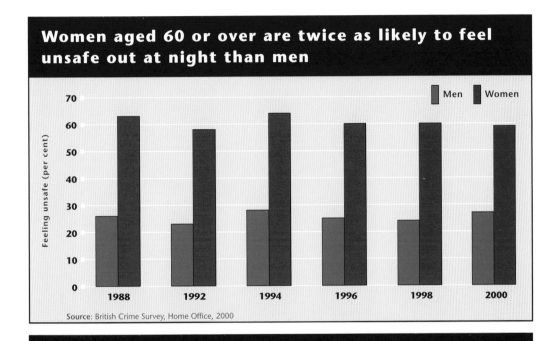

Source: British Crime Survey, Home Office, 2000

Older people who used to be in manual work are more likely to feel anxious or depressed than those from non-manual backgrounds

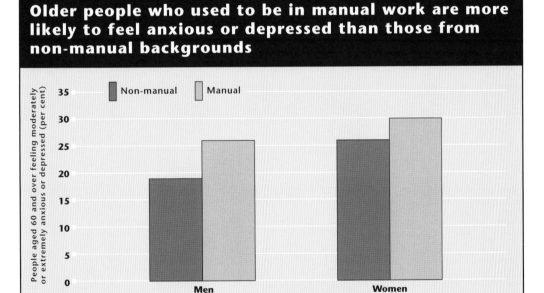

Source: Euroquol EQ-5D, published in the Health Survey for England 1996

The first graph shows the number of men and women aged 60 and over according to whether they feel safe or not walking alone in their area after dark. Those counted as feeling unsafe are those who replied that they felt 'a bit unsafe' or 'very unsafe'. The data is based on the British Crime Survey and relates to England and Wales.

The second graph shows how people aged over 60 differ in their reported levels of moderate anxiety and depression according to their occupational background.

*Overall adequacy of the indicator: **medium**. The British Crime Survey is a well-established annual government survey and the fact that the proportions feeling unsafe have changed little over successive surveys suggests a degree of robustness to this result. However, it is unclear to what extent these feelings reflect anxiety more generally or simply with respect to walking at night.*

Help from social services to live at home

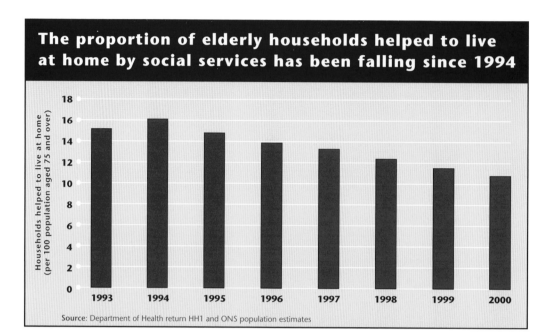

The proportion of elderly households helped to live at home by social services has been falling since 1994

Households helped to live at home (per 100 population aged 75 and over)

1993 · 1994 · 1995 · 1996 · 1997 · 1998 · 1999 · 2000

Source: Department of Health return HH1 and ONS population estimates

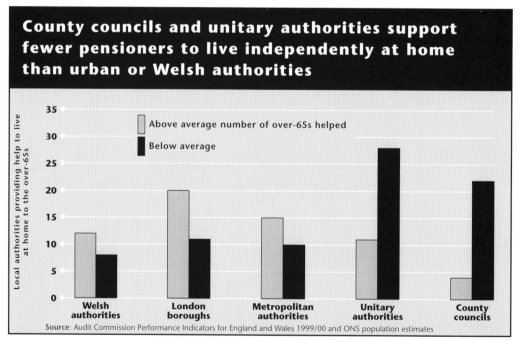

County councils and unitary authorities support fewer pensioners to live independently at home than urban or Welsh authorities

Local authorities providing help to live at home to the over-65s

Above average number of over-65s helped
Below average

Welsh authorities · London boroughs · Metropolitan authorities · Unitary authorities · County councils

Source: Audit Commission Performance Indicators for England and Wales 1999/00 and ONS population estimates

The first graph shows the proportion of households aged 75 and over receiving home help/care from their local authority. The statistics are collected by the Department of Health from all local authority social services departments in England. 'Being helped to live at home' includes provision of the following services: traditional home help services, including home help provided by volunteers; practical services which assist the client to function as independently as possible and/or continue to live in their own homes (for example routine household tasks within or outside the home); personal care of the client; shopping; respite care in support of the client's regular carers; overnight, live-in and 24-hour services. The data relates to England.

The second graph, which relates to those over 65, counts local authorities in England and Wales according to whether they help an above- or a below-average number to live at home, with the results shown by five types of authority. A small number of authorities have been omitted where the advice was that the data was unreliable.

*Overall adequacy of the indicator: **medium**. The underlying data has been collected for a number of years and can be considered reliable. However, comparisons between local authorities have to be qualified by the fact that statistics ought ideally to be measured in relation to need and levels of support from friends and relatives.*

Without a telephone

Indicator
39

The number of pensioner households without a telephone continues to fall, and now stands at around 200,000

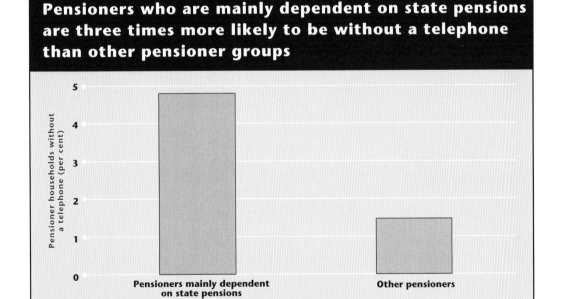

Source: Family Expenditure Survey 1999–00, ONS, © Crown Copyright 2001

Pensioners who are mainly dependent on state pensions are three times more likely to be without a telephone than other pensioner groups

Source: Family Expenditure Survey 1999–00, ONS, © Crown Copyright 2001

The first graph shows the number of pensioner households without a telephone. Pensioner households are all those where the head of household is retired: all male heads of household are 65 years of age or more; all female heads of household are 60 years of age or more.

The second graph shows how the lack of access to a telephone varies according to income. A retired household mainly dependent upon state pensions is one in which at least three-quarters of total household income is derived from national insurance retirement pension and similar pensions, and from housing and other benefits paid in supplement to or instead of the retirement pension. 'Other households' are those where more than a quarter of the household's income derives from occupational retirement pensions and/or income from investments, annuities etc.

The data relates to the United Kingdom.

Overall adequacy of the indicator: **high**. *The Family Expenditure Survey is a well-established government survey, designed to be representative of the population as a whole.*

6 Communities

Why the indicators were chosen

The indicators in this chapter cover the physical and social environment in which people live, reflecting the fact that neither poverty nor social exclusion depend upon an individual's personal resources alone.

One sense in which 'community' is used here is spatial, pertaining to the local area. A second sense is that of a network of personal contacts, from family and friends, to colleagues and, in the most abstract, fellow citizens.

Social cohesion

People's local communities can provide opportunities both for help and the chance to help.[1] The first indicator is the **'proportion of individuals who are not involved in any civic organisation'**. These range from political parties, trade unions and tenants' groups to social groups and sports clubs. The indicator shows how involvement varies across the income distribution.

The second indicator, the **'proportion of households in social housing where the head of household is not in work'**, reflects the polarisation that has taken place between areas of housing with large numbers of workless households and areas with a high proportion of two-earner households.

Gaining access is in many ways the opposite of being excluded, and the ability to travel is a crucial aspect of access. The indicator of access to transport is the **'level of expenditure on travel'**, which varies markedly across the income distribution.

Finally, it is becoming increasingly important for people to have the benefits of modern financial services, which create access to a range of other benefits and conveniences. The indicator here is the **'proportion of households which have neither a bank nor building society account'**.

Crime

Crime is the most commonly reported problem in people's neighbourhoods. In addition to the risk of crime being greater in certain types of area, some individuals and households are especially vulnerable to attack.

The first indicator shows the **'total number of burglaries'** and the greater vulnerability of particular groups to that crime.

The second indicator is **'access to insurance against crime'**, showing the variation across the income distribution in the proportion of households having home contents insurance.

The last crime indicator shows **'individuals expressing dissatisfaction with their neighbourhood'**, plus how fear of crime varies across different population groups.

Housing

The indicators in this section cover housing from a number perspectives: living conditions, availability of amenities and modernisation of housing, pressure on housing stock, and insecurity of house occupation.

The physical conditions in which people live affect their health, relations between household members, and the development of children. The first indicator is the **'proportion of households which do not have central heating'**.

Overcrowding almost invariably occurs in households with large numbers of children. It is associated with a higher rate of child accidents;[2] it encourages infection;[3] and the resulting lack of privacy can be a considerable cause of mental stress.[4] The second indicator is the '**proportion of households which are overcrowded**'.

Local authorities have a responsibility to provide accommodation for those accepted as homeless, who are given at least some form of temporary accommodation. The third housing indicator is the '**number of households living in temporary accommodation provided by a local authority**'.

Finally, mortgage debts continue to represent a problem for many people, with powerful detrimental effects on standards of living and on stress. The fourth indicator is the '**number of households over 12 months in arrears with their mortgage**'.

What the indicators show
Improving housing conditions, but greater numbers in temporary housing
Three of our housing indicators continue to improve: levels of overcrowding have almost halved in the last decade; the number of low income households without central heating has reduced by a third since 1994/95,[5] and the number of mortgage holders in serious arrears is now at its lowest level for a decade. However, these overall improvements mask continuing differences between different types of tenure: overcrowding in the social rented sector is now three times the level of those with mortgages and has not reduced over the decade,[6] and households in the private rented sector are twice as likely other households to be without central heating.[7]

In contrast, the number of households in temporary accommodation continues to rise sharply and, at 80,000, has nearly doubled since 1997. Temporary accommodation is used when a local authority accepts a family as homeless but has no social housing available for them. More than half of the households accepted by local authorities as homeless have dependent children.

There are a number of government initiatives in train to improve the quality and quantity of the housing stock, including reforms to the Housing Investment Programme and the initiative to release monies from council house sales. Whilst these initiatives do not directly cover the range of subjects in our indicators, it is worth noting that providing permanent housing for the 80,000 households currently in temporary accommodation would require an increase of less than 2 per cent in the stock of the 5 million homes in the social rented sector.

The Government has recently been focusing its attention on the subject of 'fuel poverty', which it defines as those households who spend more than 10 per cent of their disposable income on fuel. Using this definition, there are currently around 4 million households suffering from fuel poverty.[8] Insulation and central heating are viewed as two developments which can help to reduce fuel costs, and both the Home Energy Efficiency Scheme and the National Fuel Poverty Strategy[9] aim to encourage such developments, with the stated aim being to end fuel poverty in 'vulnerable' households by 2010. It remains to be seen whether the actions that these initiatives envisage for a wide variety of organisations – including industry, local government, registered social landlords and Ofgem – will be sufficient to achieve this target.

Falling crime overall, but continuing risks for the economically vulnerable
The latest British Crime Survey statistics (1999) reveal that the number of **burglaries** continues to decline and is now at its lowest level for a decade. But significant variations exist between different types of household and, for example, lone-parent households and households headed by young people (aged 16 to 24) are both three times more likely to be burgled than the average.

Households with no household insurance are around three times as likely to be burgled as those with insurance. The impact is particularly serious for those on low incomes because more than half do not have any household insurance – compared with a fifth for households on average income – and, by definition, such people are less able to replace stolen goods themselves.

Reflecting these differences, people in low income households are twice as likely to report that their quality of life is significantly affected by fear of crime than the average, and almost twice as likely to feel very dissatisfied with the area in which they live. Fear of crime is particularly common amongst Asians, a fifth of whom report that the quality of their life is greatly affected by it. Finally, 10 million people not in paid employment or full time education do not participate in any social, political, cultural or community organisations, a figure which is unchanged since a decade ago.

The Government's Crime Reduction Programme aims to reduce crime in general, and burglaries in particular, by targeting the worst areas. This is complemented by the National Strategy for Neighbourhood Renewal and the New Deal for Communities, both of which are geographically focused initiatives which aim to reduce crime in their chosen areas as part of wider regeneration. All of these initiatives are relatively recent and it remains to be seen how successful they are in reducing the disparities. None of them explicitly relate to household insurance and this is a concern given the general acceptance that 'red lining' – whereby insurance in areas with high levels of crime costs much more than in other areas – is now considered to be widespread.

No reduction in unequal access to work
In 2000/01, two-thirds of head of households in social housing did not have **paid work**, compared with one-third in other tenures. This difference has persisted throughout the last decade. It is also reflected in the relatively low incomes of social housing tenants: three-quarters live on a weekly income of less than £200, compared with a quarter of those living in other tenures; and a third live on a weekly income of less than £100, compared with 1 in 10 of those living in other tenures.

The Government has a number of initiatives aimed at improving employment prospects in selected geographic areas, including the Single Regeneration Budget, the Employment Zones and the New Deal for Communities initiative.[10] Whilst the Single Regeneration Budget has been going for a number of years, the other two initiatives are only now starting to move into implementation. As well as their overall impact on unemployment, one issue in assessing the success of these various initiatives will be the scale of the impact that they collectively have on the overall extent of worklessness in households in social housing.

No reduction in financial exclusion
In 1999/00, 1 in 6 of the poorest households did not have any type of **bank or building society account**, compared with 1 in 20 households on average incomes. These figures are unchanged from five years previously.

There is general acceptance that one of the reasons that people choose not to have a bank account is because they are not comfortable with the products currently on the market. This is despite the fact that the lack of a bank account leads to both cost and difficulty: people paying for their electricity and gas using pre-payment meters pay up to 20 per cent more,[11] employers want to pay their employees by bank transfer, and cheques can no longer be easily and cheaply cashed, except into a bank account.

In reaction, the Government has decided that the way forward lies with the introduction of basic bank accounts which cannot go overdrawn and which have no unexpected charges. They exhorted all major banks to provide such accounts by October 2000[12] and are simultaneously working with the Post Office to establish a 'universal bank'.[13] It remains to be seen how quickly and how successful these initiatives work in attracting people into the banking system.

Selected major initiatives under way

Indicators	Policy	Start date	Key department	Key delivery agency	Budget/target/comments
41 Polarisation of work	Single Regeneration Budget	1994: introduced. 1999: Round 5. 2000: Round 6. 2001: announcement that there will be no further rounds.	DTLR; interdepartmental	Regional Development Agencies	The original objectives were to improve employment prospects, address social exclusion, promote sustainable regeneration, protect the environment and infrastructure, and support and promote economic growth. From March 2001, RDAs will have more flexibility in the development of their strategies within 11 overall targets (which include a reduction of 10 per cent in the deprivation of those wards that are currently in the bottom 20 per cent of the regions identified by the Indices of Multiple Deprivation). They will meet their commitments to SRB Rounds 1 to 6 and then be able to use uncommitted resources to take forward schemes that help deliver regional strategies. Under SRB Rounds 1 to 6, there have been 900 schemes approved, worth £5.5bn in SRB support over their lifetime of up to seven years. RDA funding was boosted by 40 per cent in July 2000 and is £1.2bn in 2000/01.
	Employment Zones	February 1998: Round 1. April 2000: Round 2. February 2001: zones extended to March 2003.	DfES (DWP also involved)	Partnership of public, voluntary and private sector organisations	Each Zone is situated in an area of high unemployment and aims to get 15 to 20 per cent improvement in moving selected groups into work. A budget of £250m for 1998–2003.
	New Deal for Communities	1998: first round of 17 areas announced. 1999: 22 new areas invited to bid for funding. 2000: implementation begins in the initial 17 areas.	DTLR leads a cross-Whitehall initiative	Partnerships of local people, business, community and voluntary organisations, and local authorities. RDAs also involved	An initiative to tackle deprivation in selected areas, with the overall aims including a reduction in poor job prospects, high levels of crime, educational underachievement and poor health. Within this there are a variety of targets, including a reduction by a third between 2001 and 2004 in the number of households living in social housing that does not meet defined standards. Each initiative focuses on a small geographic area of up to 4,000 households, with a 10-year timeframe, funding of £20m to £50m, and some local flexibility in how the money is spent. A budget of £800 million over 1999–2002, with a ten-year commitment to £2bn.
	National Strategy for Neighbourhood Renewal	2001 strategy published and Neighbourhood Renewal Unit established.	Neighbourhood Renewal Unit leads a cross-Whitehall initiative	Lead government department varies by subject area	Two overall aims: first, to bridge the gap between the most deprived neighbourhoods and the rest of England; and second, to achieve lower long-term worklessness, less crime, better health and better educational qualifications in the worst neighbourhoods. It provides an overall strategy covering such schemes as the New Deals, SureStart, Connexions and the Employment Zones. Within this, there are a variety of targets including: (1) no district to have a burglary rate more than three times the national average; (2) no LEA to have fewer than 38 per cent of pupils achieving five GCSEs at A* toC, and no school to have fewer than 25 per cent of pupils getting five GCSEs A* to C by 2004; (3) to raise employment rates in the 30 local authority districts with the poorest initial labour market position to narrow the gap between these areas and overall rates; (4) to reduce by 33 per cent the number of households living in non-decent social housing by 2004, with the most improvement going to the most deprived areas; and (5) to narrow health inequalities between social and economic groups and between the most deprived areas and the rest of the country. £800 million will be paid to the Neighbourhood Renewal Fund to help the 88 most deprived districts over 2001 to 2004, with additional funding of £40m to support Local Strategic Partnerships and £50m to support the Community Chest.

Indicators	Policy	Start date	Key department	Key delivery agency	Budget/target/comments
43 Without a bank account	Basic bank accounts	October 2000: all banks to have such accounts.	Treasury	Banks and building societies	A general exhortation to all major banks to provide basic bank accounts, with no overdraft facilities, by October 2000.
	Universal bank	2001: announced.	DTI	The Post Office and individual post offices	A joint initiative between the government and the Post Office to provide access to basic bank accounts at post offices. Funding arrangements are not currently public but are likely to include a substantial contribution from government as well as from the major banks.
44 Burglaries	Crime reduction programme	April 1999: initiated. Individual projects have varying start dates.	Home Office	Police, and prison service	An umbrella scheme covering 15 separate projects aimed at the Government's general crime reduction targets. A particular target is to reduce domestic burglary by 25 per cent from the 1998/99 baseline, with no local authorities having a rate more than 3 times the national average by 2005. A budget of £250m for 2000–03, with a further £153m announced for the CCTV initiative.
	Reducing Burglary Initiative	April 1999: Round 1. October 1999: Round 2. April 2000: Round 3.	Home Office	Local partnerships	Aims to reduce burglary nationally by targeting areas with the worst domestic burglary problems. Round 1 and 2 applicants needed to have a level of burglaries twice the national average and were limited to a one-year duration. Round 3 applicants must have levels of burglaries 1½ times the national average and are no longer limited in their duration. Between 1999 and 2002, 2 million homes will be covered. A budget of £25m.
	New Deal for Communities	See above	See above	See above	See above
	National Strategy for Neighbourhood Renewal	See above	See above	See above	See above
47 Without central heating	Home Energy Efficiency Scheme	May 2000: introduced.	DTLR	HEES referral networks: local authorities, health bodies and voluntary groups	Aims to improve heating and insulation of vulnerable households through grants of up to £2,000. Focused on the private sector. Estimated to help around 800,000 fuel-poor households by 2004. A budget of £600m for 2000-04.
	UK Fuel Poverty Strategy	February 2001: consultation draft.	DTLR	DTLR and devolved administrations	Aims to improve energy efficiency and reduce the costs of fuel for fuel-poor households, with a target of ending fuel poverty in vulnerable households by 2010 in the UK. Other households will be addressed after progress is made on vulnerable households. No specific budget.
48 Overcrowding	Housing Investment Programme reforms	Gradual.	DTLR	Local authorities	A variety of targets, including: (1) by March 2002, to reduce the backlog of council house repairs by at least 250,000, with more than 1.5million council houses benefiting from the new investment by March 2002; and (2) to reduce the number of people sleeping rough by two-thirds from current levels by 2002. An overall budgetary allocation of £2.65bn in 2001/02 (HIP = £0.98bn, MRA = £1.67bn) and £2.55bn in 2002/03.
	The Capital Receipts Initiative to release council house sale monies	1997	DTLR	Local authorities	Aims include tackling poor housing and poor health in run-down estates. A budget of £1.3bn over the three years to 1999/00.

Non-participation in civic organisations

Indicator
40

Ten million adults who are not in paid work or full-time education do not participate in any social, political, cultural or community organisations

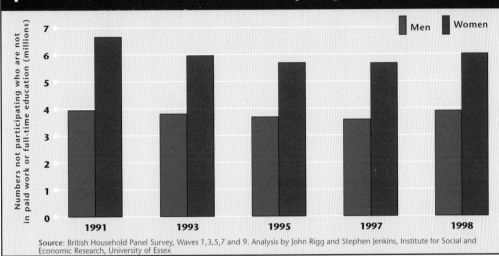

Source: British Household Panel Survey, Waves 1,3,5,7 and 9. Analysis by John Rigg and Stephen Jenkins, Institute for Social and Economic Research, University of Essex

The poorest are much less likely to participate in social, political or community organisations than the richest

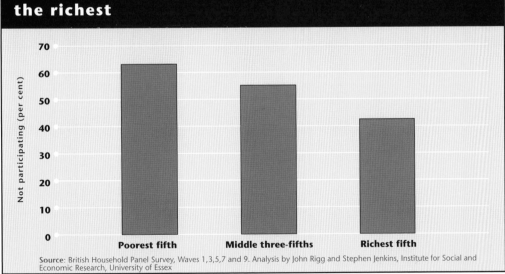

Source: British Household Panel Survey, Waves 1,3,5,7 and 9. Analysis by John Rigg and Stephen Jenkins, Institute for Social and Economic Research, University of Essex

The first graph shows the number of individuals over the age of 16 who are not in work and who report themselves as being active in none of a range of social and other organisations.

The second graph shows the percentages of all those over 16 not active in any of these organisations, with results shown separately for those in the lowest, highest and middle three-fifths of the income distribution.

The social and other organisations are: trade unions and professional associations, parents' associations, pensioner groups, community and tenant groups, women's groups, religious groups, sports and social groups, and political parties. Income is net household income (note: gross income was used last year), equivalised for household membership. The data comes from the British Household Panel Survey and the results relate to Great Britain.

*Overall adequacy of the indicator: **medium**. The British Household Panel Survey is a smaller survey than Family Resources Survey. Coupled with concern over the gradual fall in the number of respondents, it is felt that less weight can be placed on results from this source*

Polarisation of work

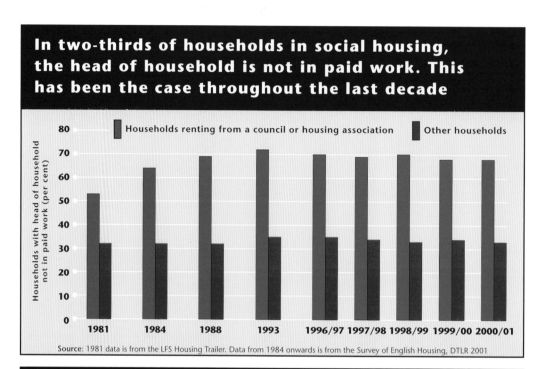

In two-thirds of households in social housing, the head of household is not in paid work. This has been the case throughout the last decade

Source: 1981 data is from the LFS Housing Trailer. Data from 1984 onwards is from the Survey of English Housing, DTLR 2001

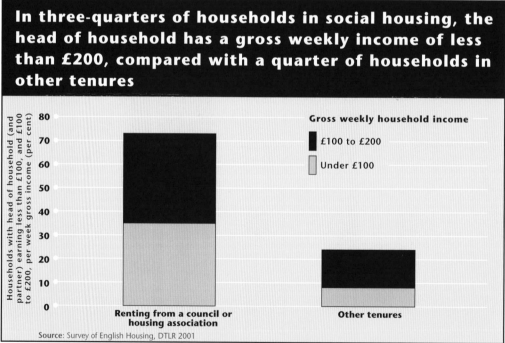

In three-quarters of households in social housing, the head of household has a gross weekly income of less than £200, compared with a quarter of households in other tenures

Source: Survey of English Housing, DTLR 2001

The first graph shows the percentage of households by tenure group where the head of household (and partner, if any) is in neither full nor part time work. Two figures are given for each year: the percentage of households in the social rented sector where the head is not in full or part time work; and the percentage for all other tenures.

For the same two tenure groups, the second graph shows the percentage of households where the gross weekly income of the head of household and their partner is less than £100, plus the percentage where the gross household income lies between £100 and £200. These percentages are for 2000/01.

The graphs relate to England only.

Overall adequacy of the indicator: **high.** *The Survey of English Housing is a well-established annual government survey, designed to be nationally representative.*

Spending on travel

Households on average incomes spend four times as much on travel as households with the lowest incomes

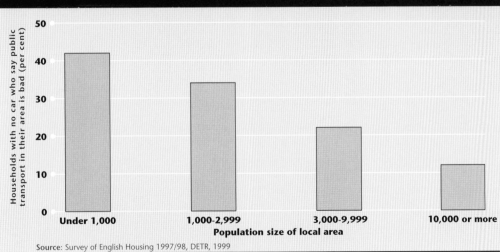

■ Poorest fifth of income distribution ■ Middle fifth of income distribution

£s per week spent on motoring, fares and other travel costs (April 2000 prices)

1993/94 1994/95 1995/96 1996/97 1997/98 1998/99 1999/00

Source: Family Expenditure Survey 1999–00, ONS, © Crown Copyright 2001

40 per cent of households without a car living in rural areas say that their public transport is bad compared with only 12 per cent living in large towns and cities

Households with no car who say public transport in their area is bad (per cent)

Under 1,000   1,000-2,999   3,000-9,999   10,000 or more
Population size of local area

Source: Survey of English Housing 1997/98, DETR, 1999

The first graph shows weekly household spending on travel for two representative households: for a 'poorer' household at the 10th percentile of the income distribution (i.e. 10 per cent of households received an income below that value); and for a household with average income (i.e. at the 50th percentile of the income distribution).

Two categories of spending are included: 'motoring' and 'fares and other travel costs'. The data is at current year prices. Income is gross weekly household income. The figures relate to the United Kingdom.

The second graph shows the percentage of households who do not have access to a car, who said public transport was bad in their area. These answers were obtained from a special question asked in the Survey of English Housing in 1997/8. The results are for England only.

Overall adequacy of the indicator: **high.** *The Family Expenditure Survey and the Survey of English Housing are both well-established annual government surveys, designed to be nationally representative.*

Without a bank or building society account

Indicator
43

One in six of the poorest households still do not have any type of bank/building society account, compared with one in twenty households on average incomes

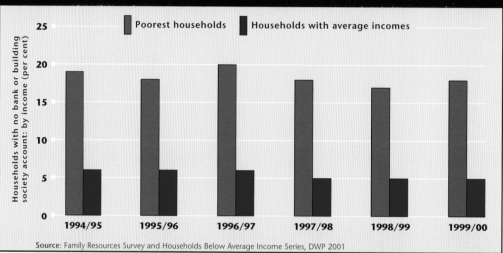

Source: Family Resources Survey and Households Below Average Income Series, DWP 2001

Households where the head is unemployed or either Bangladeshi or Pakistani are twice as likely to have no account as the average household. Lone parent households are over three times as likely

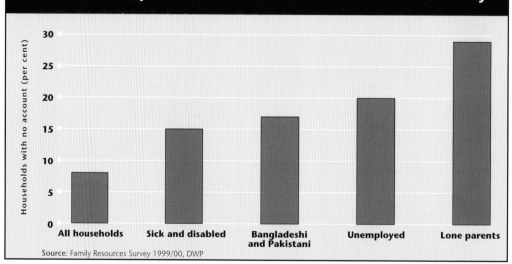

Source: Family Resources Survey 1999/00, DWP

The first graph shows the percentage of households in each fifth of the income distribution without any kind of bank, building society or any other kind of account. Income is household disposable income, equivalised to take account of household composition, and is measured before housing costs.

The second graph shows the percentages of different households in the population without any kind of account. A figure for all households is provided for comparison.

As well as bank, building society and post office accounts, the figures also count any stocks and shares, premium bonds, gilts and Save As You Earn arrangements. The results relate to Great Britain.

Note that care should be taken with the data, with year on year fluctuations for particular groups potentially due to small sample sizes.

*Overall adequacy of the indicator: **medium**. The Family Resources Survey is probably the most representative of the surveys that gather information on the extent to which people have bank and other types of account. The qualification is that the extent to which access to any kind of account is a proper measure of how far people have the banking services they need is not clear.*

Burglaries

Indicator
44

The number of burglaries continues to decline, although it is still higher than in the 1980s

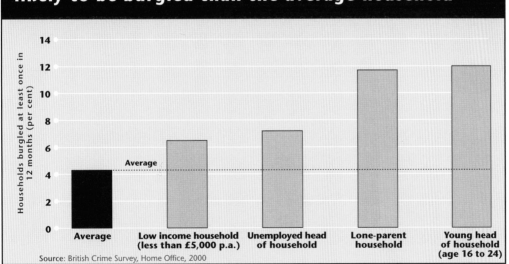

Source: British Crime Survey, Home Office, 2000

Lone-parent and young households are much more likely to be burgled than the average household

Source: British Crime Survey, Home Office, 2000

The first graph shows the number of burglaries committed in Britain in each year shown, according to the British Crime Survey.

The second graph, again from the British Crime Survey, shows the vulnerability to burglary of different household types, set against the national average.

*Overall adequacy of the indicator: **high**. The British Crime Survey is a well-established government survey, which is designed to be nationally representative.*

Without household insurance

Indicator
45

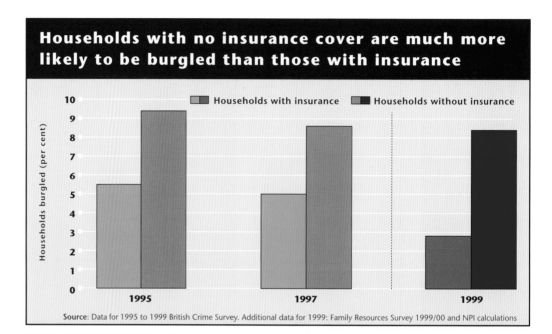

Households with no insurance cover are much more likely to be burgled than those with insurance

Households with insurance   Households without insurance

Households burgled (per cent)

1995   1997   1999

Source: Data for 1995 to 1999 British Crime Survey. Additional data for 1999: Family Resources Survey 1999/00 and NPI calculations

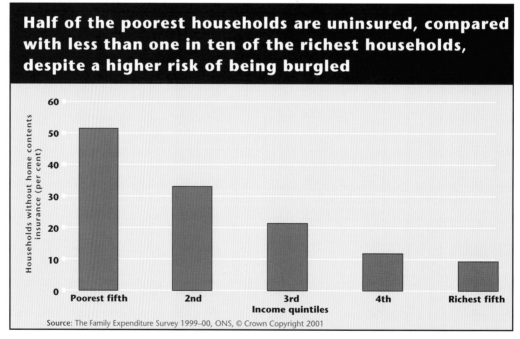

Half of the poorest households are uninsured, compared with less than one in ten of the richest households, despite a higher risk of being burgled

Households without home contents insurance (per cent)

Poorest fifth   2nd   3rd   4th   Richest fifth
Income quintiles

Source: The Family Expenditure Survey 1999–00, ONS, © Crown Copyright 2001

The first graph shows the percentage of households with, and without, home contents insurance that were victims of a burglary one or more times in each of the years shown. The data for 1995 and 1997 is taken directly from the British Crime Survey (BCS). The rate for 1999 is calculated using data on burglaries from the BCS and data on household insurance from the Family Resources Survey (FRS). This is due to the BCS discontinuing a direct question on this topic in their survey. Data for 1999 is therefore not directly comparable with previous years' data.

The second graph shows how the percentage of households without insurance cover for household contents varies according to the household's income. It is based on Family Expenditure Survey (FES) data. The data is for the UK, and the definition of income is gross weekly household income.

*Overall adequacy of the indicator: **medium**. Data for the latest year of the first graph is taken from the BCS and the FRS, and is based on our own calculation. The BCS, FRS and FES are well-established government surveys, which are designed to be nationally representative.*

Dissatisfaction with local area

Low income households are much more likely to feel very dissatisfied with the area they live in than households on average

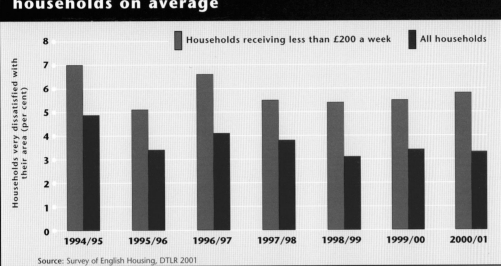

Households receiving less than £200 a week ▮ All households

Households very dissatisfied with their area (per cent)

Source: Survey of English Housing, DTLR 2001

Asians are three times more likely to report that their quality of life is greatly affected by the fear of crime than people on average

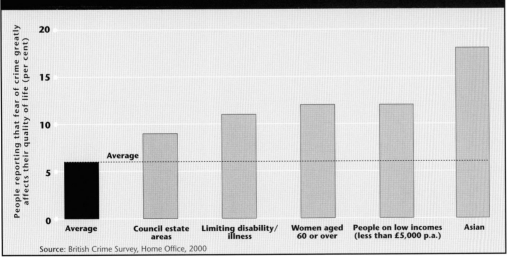

People reporting that fear of crime greatly affects their quality of life (per cent)

Average

Average | Council estate areas | Limiting disability/ illness | Women aged 60 or over | People on low incomes (less than £5,000 p.a.) | Asian

Source: British Crime Survey, Home Office, 2000

The first graph shows the proportion of households saying they are very dissatisfied with their local area, with separate results for those with a gross weekly household income below £200 and for all households.

'Household income' is the income of the head of household and their partner. The figures count those who replied 'very dissatisfied' to the question, the lowest of five possible responses. The data relates to England.

The second graph shows the percentage of different groups in the population who report that fear of crime affects their quality of life. The data is based on the 2000 British Crime Survey.

Overall adequacy of the indicator: **high.** *The Survey of English Housing and the British Crime Survey are both well-established government surveys, designed to be nationally representative.*

Without central heating

**Indicator
47**

The proportion of low income households without central heating continues to fall steadily, although they are still much more likely to be without it than households on average incomes

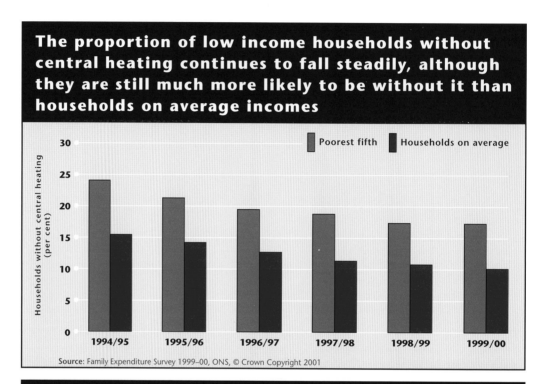

Source: Family Expenditure Survey 1999–00, ONS, © Crown Copyright 2001

Those living in the private rented sector are the most likely to be without central heating

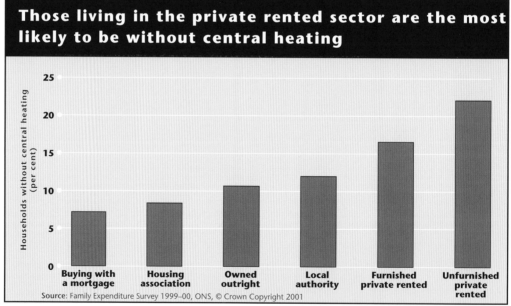

Source: Family Expenditure Survey 1999–00, ONS, © Crown Copyright 2001

The first graph shows the percentage of households without central heating, with separate figures given for the poorest fifth of households and for households on average.

The second graph breaks down the 2000/01 figures according to household tenure.

Income is gross weekly household income. The results relate to the United Kingdom.

*Overall adequacy of the indicator: **high**. The Family Expenditure Survey is a well-established, regular government survey, designed to be nationally representative.*

Overcrowding

Indicator
48

The proportion of households which are overcrowded continues to decline

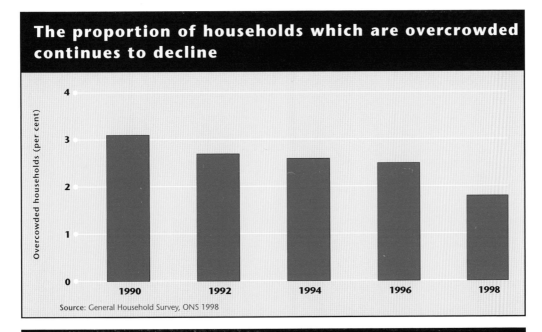

Source: General Household Survey, ONS 1998

Overcrowding is much more prevalent in rented housing than in owner-occupation

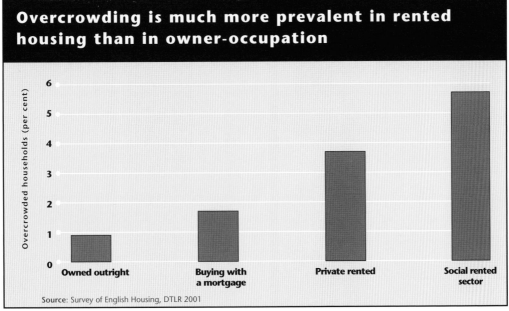

Source: Survey of English Housing, DTLR 2001

The first graph shows the percentage of households that fall below a measure of occupation density known as the 'bedroom standard'. The 'bedroom standard' is calculated in relation to the number of bedrooms and the number of household members and their relationship to each other. One bedroom is allocated to each married or cohabiting couple, any other person over 21, each pair aged 10 to 20 of the same sex and each pair of children under 10.

The data relates to Great Britain.

The second graph shows the percentage of households overcrowded by tenure for 2000–01 using the same standard.

*Overall adequacy of the indicator: **limited**. The bedroom standard itself is low, particularly for those aged over 10, and the overall level of overcrowding shown by it may therefore be too low. Due to an insufficient degree of accuracy in the published data, the values for individual years shown in the first graph are to be regarded as illustrative only.*

Households in temporary accommodation

Indicator
49

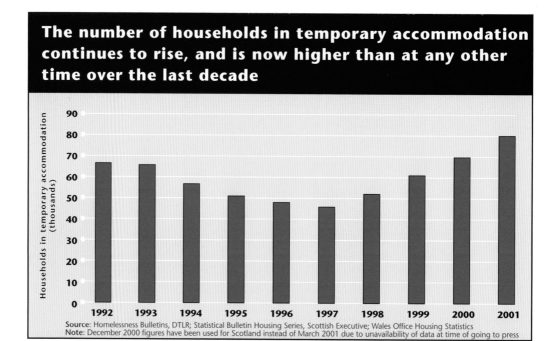

The number of households in temporary accommodation continues to rise, and is now higher than at any other time over the last decade

Households in temporary accommodation (thousands)

Source: Homelessness Bulletins, DTLR; Statistical Bulletin Housing Series, Scottish Executive; Wales Office Housing Statistics
Note: December 2000 figures have been used for Scotland instead of March 2001 due to unavailability of data at time of going to press

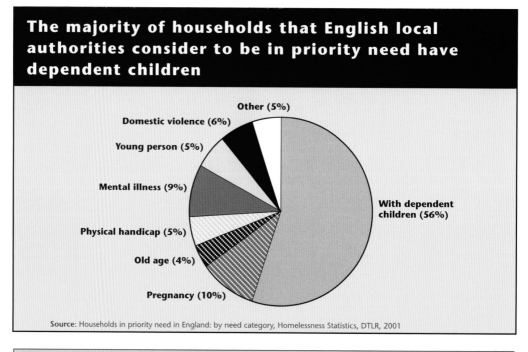

The majority of households that English local authorities consider to be in priority need have dependent children

Source: Households in priority need in England: by need category, Homelessness Statistics, DTLR, 2001

The first graph shows the number of households in temporary accommodation in Great Britain, measured at the end of the first quarter of each year. 'Temporary accommodation' includes bed and breakfast, hostel accommodation, private renting, and other. For 2001, first quarter data was not available for Scotland, so it was assumed that levels were the same as the last quarter of the previous year (2000).

Note that, since 1996, local authorities have had an obligation to house asylum seekers appealing against an asylum decision and this has put increased pressure on temporary housing. Also note that Scottish temporary accommodation statistics were revised in 2001 by the Scottish Executive from 1993 onwards.

The second graph shows the breakdown of households that were accepted by local authorities in England as being homeless in the first quarter of 2001 according to the reason why the household was accepted as being in priority need.

*Overall adequacy of the indicator: **limited**. While there is no reason to believe there is any problem with the underlying data, the extent to which it leaves 'homelessness' dependent on administrative definition is clearly unsatisfactory. In particular, the figures do not include any single people, towards whom local authorities have no general duty.*

Mortgage arrears

The number of mortgage holders in serious arrears continues to fall

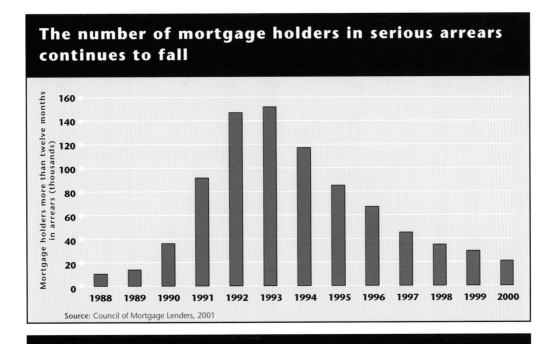

Source: Council of Mortgage Lenders, 2001

One in seven working age heads of households with a mortgage is in an economically vulnerable position – in part-time work, unemployed or economically inactive

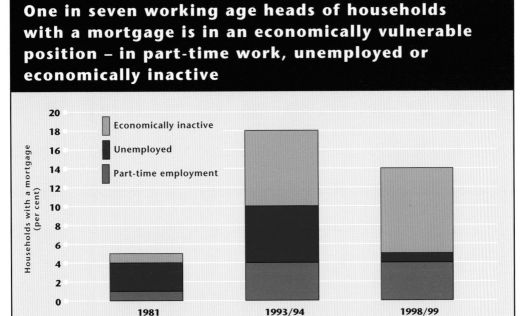

Source: 1981 – LFS Housing Trailer, DoE, 1993/94–2000/01 – Survey of English Housing; DTLR 2001

The first graph shows the number of residential mortgage holders who were 12 months or more in arrears with their mortgage repayments. The data relates to the United Kingdom. Figures are based on the statistics provided by a sample of members of the Council of Mortgage lenders. Figures are based on a sample of approximately 88 per cent and are grossed up to represent the whole of CML membership, which accounts for around 98 per cent of the total mortgage lending market.

The second graph shows the economic status of the heads of households with mortgages. It is based on the Survey of English Housing and relates to England only.

*Overall adequacy of the indicator: **high**. The data for the first graph is produced regularly by the CML from surveys among their members. The data for the second graph is from a well-established government survey designed to be nationally representative.*

References

Chapter 1 Income

1   Hills, J., *Income and Wealth: The Latest Evidence*, Joseph Rowntree Foundation, 1998. Both statistics relate to the number of households who said that they 'did not have and could not afford' particular items from a list of items deemed necessities by a majority of the population at the time.

2   The year-on-year changes during the 1990s are smaller than the statistical uncertainties in the Family Resources Survey on which the calculations are based.

3   A two-and-a-half-fold rise during the 1980s, followed by little change during the 1990s.

Note that the increases in the numbers of the very poorest during the 1980s are more extreme when monitored using mean income as opposed to median: a quadrupling for the mean, compared with a trebling for the median.

Also note that, whilst the numbers below 60 per cent of median income did not change during the 1990s, the numbers below 50 per cent of the mean, if anything, drifted upwards (from 13.2 million in 1991/92 to 14.0 in 1999/00). One reason for this could be that the incomes of the more wealthy in society have been rising faster than the incomes of the less wealthy (given that the former only changes mean income and not median income).

4   The table below summarises the figures upon which these two statements are based.

	below 50% of mean (millions)	below 40% of mean (millions)		below 60% of median (millions)	below 50% of median (millions)
1979/80	5.2	1.9	1979	7.1	3.1
1980/81	5.8	2.1			
1981/82	5.9	2.0	1981	8.1	3.6
1982/83	5.9	2.1			
1983/84	6.3	2.3			
1984/85	7.0	2.5			
1985/86	8.2	3.1			
1986/87	9.5	4.0			
1987/88	10.8	5.2	1987	11.1	5.8
1988/89	11.7	6.0	1988/89	12.6	7.6
1989/90	12.4	6.8			
1990/91	13.2	7.5	1990/91	13.5	8.7
1991/92	13.6	7.7	1991/92	13.9	9
1992/93	13.7	7.8	1992/93	13.9	8.9
1993/94	13.3	7.5	1993/94	13.5	8.5
1994/95	13.3	7.3	1994/95	13.1	8.1
1995/96	13.3	7.1	1995/96	12.9	7.7
1996/97	14.1	8.2	1996/97	13.9	9
1997/98	14.0	8.4	1997/98	13.5	8.9
1998/99	14.3	8.7	1998/99	13.4	8.8
1999/00	14.0	8.3	1999/00	13.3	8.7

5   For example, see Bradshaw, J. (ed.), *Household Budgets and Living Standards,* Joseph Rowntree Foundation, 1993. Also see Gordon, D. et al., *Poverty and Social Exclusion In Britain,* Joseph Rowntree Foundation, 2000.

6   There are also certain methodological issues relating to whether such indicators are understandable, how 'essential' is defined and the risk that the result is claimed to be a 'scientifically correct' measure of the numbers of people in the UK who are 'in poverty'.

7   The table below is taken from Appendix 2, *Households Below Half Average Income 1994/5–1999/00*, DWP 2001, where further details of equivalisation are also discussed.

HBAI Equivalence Scale Variants (Couples are taken as the reference point and given an equivalence value of 1).

	After housing costs	Before housing costs
Head	0.55	0.61
Spouse	0.45	0.39
Other second adult	0.45	0.46
Third adult	0.45	0.42
Subsequent adults	0.40	0.36
Each dependant aged:		
0–1	0.07	0.09
2–4	0.18	0.18
5–7	0.21	0.21
8–10	0.23	0.23
11–12	0.26	0.25
13–15	0.28	0.27
16 and over	0.38	0.36

Chapter 2 Children

1   Spencer, N., *Poverty and Child Health*, Radcliffe Press, 1996, page 112; Carr-Hill, R., 'The measurement of inequalities in health: lessons from the British experience', *Social Science and Medicine*, 31(3), 1990, pages 393–404; Botting, B. (ed.) *The Health of our Children*, Decennial Supplement Series DS No. 11, 1995, page 71.

2   Jarvis, S., Towner, E. and Walsh, S., in Botting, B. (ed.) *The Health of our Children*, Decennial Supplement Series DS No. 11, 1995, page 95.

3   *The Health of Children in Wales*, The Welsh Office, 1997, page 49.

4   Machin, S., in *Exclusion, Employment and Opportunity*, CASE Paper No 4, Atkinson, A. and Hills, J. (eds), 1998, page 61.

5   Donovan, N. (ed.) *Second Chances: Exclusion From School and Equality of Opportunity*, New Policy Institute, 1998.

6   Note that young people in care are estimated to make up a third of all secondary school exclusions and two-thirds of all primary school exclusions: Smith, R., *No Lessons Learnt*, The Children's Society, 1998.

7   Health Advisory Service (1995) and Health Committee (1997), cited in Malek, M., *Nurturing Healthy Minds*, National Children's Bureau, 1997, table 1 page 10.

8   *The Health of Children in Wales,* The Welsh Office, 1997, page 29.

9   Many young teenage mothers drop out of school early: Gustavsson, N. and Segal, E., *Critical Issues in Child Welfare*, Sage Publications, 1994, page 26. More than half never resume their education, even though they are below the statutory school leaving age: *The Needs and Cares of Adolescents*, British Paediatric Association, 1985, page 20.

10 In 1993, 89 per cent of young offenders were re-convicted within two years: *Criminal Statistics, England and Wales 1996,* Home Office, 1996, page 48.

11 After Housing Costs, excluding the self-employed. Department of Social Security, *Households Below Average Income 1994/95–1999/00*, Department of Social Security, 2001, Table 5.2.

12 The 1999/00 figures are based on survey data from October/November 1999. In our 1999 report, we presented a model that we had developed to estimate the effects of various policy and economic variables on the number on low income. This model included an estimate of between 120,000 and 180,000 fewer people on low income for every 20 per cent rise in child benefit. This equates to around 60,000 to 90,000 fewer children in low income households. In April 1999, child benefit for the eldest child was increased to £14.40 (a £2.50, or 21 per cent increase above inflation). There were also some increases in income support for recipients with children in November 1998, and the national minimum wage was introduced in April 1999.

13   *Opportunity for All: one year on: making a difference,* DWP, 2000.

14   Some of the Government's policies for increasing the income of low income families with children apply to all families (for example child benefit increases); others only apply to families in work (for example working families tax credit, national minimum wage), whilst others only apply to families not in work (for example increases in income support for recipients with children).

15   Figures for 2000/01 will not be available until November 2001.

16   *A League Table of Child Deaths by Injury in Rich Nations,* Innocenti Report Card No. 2, UNICEF, February 2001.

17   For example, *Teenage Pregnancy,* Stationery Office, June 1999 states that rates of teenage pregnancy are currently six times as high as in Holland and three times as high as in France.

Chapter 3 Young adults
1   Dennehy, L. Smith, and Harker, P., *Not To Be Ignored: Young people, poverty and health,* Child Poverty Action Group, 1997, foreword.

2   Rushton, S., *Children in Europe,* NCH Action for Children, 1996, page 268.

3   Kelly, S. and Bunting, J., *Trends in Suicide in England and Wales 1982–1996,* ONS Population Trends, 1998.

4   Fletcher, DR., Woodhill, D. and Herrington, A., 'Employment and training for ex-offenders', *Findings* Ref. 628, Joseph Rowntree Foundation, 1998.

5   The Labour Force Survey data suggests that the unemployment rate for 16- and 17-year-olds is even higher, but given the high proportion of this age group who are in education this percentage may not be completely reliable.

6   This issue is discussed further in the chapter on adults. In essence, the Office for National Statistics have declared the low pay data in both the Labour Force Survey and the New Earnings Survey to be unreliable, and thus outside researchers now have to rely on whatever data the Office decides to publish. Currently, the published data only provides breakdowns for the age groups 18 to 21 and 22+, and only for the years 1998 to 2000.

7   It is not clear who these 50,000 people are and how it is that they appear to be earning less than the legal minimum. It may well be that most come from those groups who are exempt from the minimum wage legislation, as listed in the adults chapter.

Chapter 4 Adults
1   Department of Social Security, *Social Security Statistics 1997,* Stationery Office, 1997, page 43.

2   The long-term unemployed are 50 per cent more likely to die of lung cancer and other respiratory diseases than people in secure work: Drever, F. and Whitehead, M., *Health Inequalities,* ONS, 1998.

3   For example, even those with quite modest qualifications averaged 20 per cent more in hourly earnings than those with no qualifications at all: *How Education and Training Make Work Pay for Lone Mothers,* DfEE, 1997.

4   McCormick, J., in *Welfare in Working Order,* IPPR, 1998, page 177.

5   'Introduction' booklet, Depression Alliance, 1995, page 10. A poor working environment and social isolation are also factors which heighten the risk of depressive illness.

6   Government targets for the numbers into work from the various New Deal initiatives are as follows (thousands).

Initiative	1999/00	2000/01	2001/02	Total
Long-term unemployed	38	32	62	132
Disabled people	85	1	5	91
Lone parents	15	29	62	106
Over 50s		14	30	44
Partners of unemployed people		3	3	6
Total	138	79	162	379

7   Presumably, the 1/4 million employees being paid less than the minimum wage are from groups which are exempt from this legislation. For national minimum wage purposes, a 'worker' is someone who has a contract of employment, or someone who does work personally for someone else (under a 'worker's contract') and is not genuinely self-employed. The contract does not have to be written – it may be an oral contract, or it may be implied. The following groups are exempted from the minimum wage:
* the self-employed
* voluntary workers, where voluntary workers are classified as those who have no contractual agreement and who receive no payment or payment in kind
* some trainees on government-funded schemes or on programmes supported by the European Social Fund
* some apprentices
* people living and working within a family who share in the work and leisure activities of the household (e.g. au pairs, nannies and companions)
* students doing work experience as part of a higher education course
* company directors
* members of the armed forces
* share fishermen (those who do not receive a fixed wage or salary but who agree to divide up amongst themselves the proceeds or profits from a catch)
* prisoners

8   For example, as stated in *The National Minimum Wage: Third Report of the Low Pay Commission* Volume I, 2001, Appendix 1: 'The Labour Force Survey (LFS) and the New Earnings Survey (NES) each produce biased estimates of the numbers in low pay for different reasons. The NES under-samples individuals earning less than PAYE thresholds, and therefore understates the level of low pay. The LFS suffers from problems of bias in its estimation of hourly earnings, which lead to an understatement of hourly earnings, and produce much higher estimates of numbers on low pay than the NES.'

9   Statistics utilising the Spring 2001 Labour Force Survey are expected to be published on 26 October 2001.

Chapter 5 Older people

1   Pensioners receiving the state earnings related pensions are not included in this group. Note that, although pensioners relying solely on state benefits are obviously the worst off in their age group, many of those with investment income or second pensions have little extra from these sources.

2   Department of Health, *Our Healthier Nation: A contract for health,* Stationery Office, 1998, page 8.

3   *Telecommunications services for people with disabilities – Response by Age Concern,* Briefing Paper 0798, 1998.

4   Clark, H., Dyer, S. and Horwood, J., 'The importance of "low level" preventive services to older people', Joseph Rowntree Foundation *Findings* Ref. 768, 1998.

5   From the Omnibus Survey in 2000, 71 per cent of those survey believed that a telephone was a necessity. Gordon, D., et al., *Poverty and Social Exclusion In Britain,* Joseph Rowntree Foundation, 2000.

6   When introduced in April 1999, the minimum income guarantee was £75 a week for single pensioners and £116.60 for couples. These figures represent increases of around £4 and £7 per week respectively compared with the levels of income support that applied previously.

7   In April 2000, the minimum income guarantee was raised to £78.45 for single pensioners and £121.95 for pensioner couples, representing increases of £3.45 and £5.35 over the previous year. In April 2001, it was raised to £92.15 for single pensioners and £140.55 for couples, representing increases of £13.70 and £18.60 over the previous year.

The table below compares the April 2001 figures with two thresholds of low income: half average income and those in *Low Cost But Acceptable Incomes For Older People*, Parker, H. (ed.) 2000.

	Minimum income guarantee (from April 2001)	60% of median income (1999/00, Before Housing Costs)	'Low cost but acceptable'
Singles	£92	£107	£123
Couples	£141	£175	£184

One of the characteristics of the minimum income guarantee is that large numbers of pensioners will be on the same level of income. Depending on the level of this income and the level of the low income thresholds with which it is compared, either the numbers below the threshold substantially reduced in April 2001 or they were largely unchanged. This illustrates the problem in using a single low income threshold when making assessments about what is happening to income poverty.

8   At the time of writing, the latest available official estimates of take-up were for 1998/99, which pre-dates the minimum income guarantee. These figures suggest a take-up of income support in the range of 70 to 80 per cent of those eligible. Official take-up figures for 1999/00 are currently expected to be available in December 2001.

Chapter 6 Communities

1   Humm J., 1997, *Progress Report of the Community Sector Observatory*, Community Development Foundation, 1997.

2   NCVCCO 1995, *No Fault Of Their Own*, cited in NCH Action for Children '98 *Factfile*, page 164.

3   Woodruffe, C., Glickman, M., Barker, M. and Power, C., *Children, Teenagers and Health: the Key Data*, OUP, 1993, page 105.

4   Barrett, S., *Health Prospects for Young Citizens of the North West*, Department of Public Health, Liverpool University, 1998.

5   An alternative, less strict, measure used by John Hills shows a small increase from 1990 to 1994. This measure is, however, more to do with 'density' than overcrowding as it is based on households where there are 1+ persons per room, and John Hills has confirmed to us that our measure is a preferable indicator of overcrowding.

6   The percentage of overcrowded households in the social rented sector, using the same definition of overcrowded as indicator 48, is:

1988	1991	1993/94	1994/95	1995/96	1996/97	1997/98	1998/99	1999/00	2000/01
5.5%	7.0%	5.6%	5.2%	4.5%	5.0%	4.9%	4.5%	5.5%	5.7%

Note: Data for 1993/94 onwards in the table above is from the Survey of English Housing. Data for 1988 and 1991 is from the Labour Force Survey.

7   Although, interestingly, the proportion of households in the social rented sector who are without central heating is similar to that of owner-occupiers. The percentage of households without central heating, using data from the Family Expenditure Survey, is:

	Private rented (%)	Other (%)
1994–95	29	14
1995–96	33	12
1996–97	27	11
1997–98	26	10
1998–99	25	9
1999–2000	19	10

8   As illustrated in the table below, around 60 per cent of households in fuel poverty are in the private sector (owner-occupied or rented) and 40 per cent in the social rented sector. As a share of each sector, however, only about one-fifth of all private sector properties are fuel poor, compared with one-third of all social rented sector properties.

Households in fuel poverty: England, Scotland and Wales (1999)

Millions	Vulnerable households	Other households	Total
Social rented sector	1.2	0.5	1.7
Private sector (rent and own)	1.7	0.7	2.4
Total	2.8	1.2	4.0

The figures in this table are a composite of published figures for England (which give this breakdown) and row totals for Wales and Scotland for 1996, factored down in line with estimates of the reduction in the number of UK fuel poor between 1996 and 1999, and allocated between columns in line with the proportions for England).

9   *UK Fuel Poverty Strategy – consultation document*, DTLR, February 2001.

10   Clearly, the Government's various New Deal initiatives aimed at reducing unemployment are also relevant to this indicator.

11   Figures for 1999 show pre-payment electricity bills £27 (11 per cent) and pre-payment gas prices £51 (19 per cent) higher. *OFGEM Social Action Plan*, March 2000, Appendix D2 and *OFGEM Social Action Plan Annual Review*, March 2001, Appendix 1.

12   See, for example, *Access to Financial Services*, PAT 14 report, HM Treasury, 1999.

13   See, for example, *Counter Revolution*, Performance Innovation Unit, 2000.